BRITAIN'S RAILWAYS THROUGH THE SEASONS

Start dates of the astronomical seasons

Spring: 20 March
Summer: 20 June
Autumn: 22 September
Winter: 21 December

BRITAIN'S RAILWAYS THROUGH THE SEASONS

ICONIC SCENES OF TRAINS AND ARCHITECTURE

David Goodyear

AN IMPRINT OF PEN & SWORD BOOKS LTD.
YORKSHIRE – PHILADELPHIA

First published in Great Britain in 2022 by
Pen and Sword Transport
An imprint of
Pen & Sword Books Ltd.
Yorkshire - Philadelphia

Copyright © David Goodyear, 2022

ISBN 978 1 39908 650 9

The right of David Goodyear to be identified as Author of this work has been asserted by him in accordance with the Copyright, Designs and Patents Act 1988.

A CIP catalogue record for this book is available from the British Library.

All rights reserved. No part of this book may be reproduced or transmitted in any form or by any means, electronic or mechanical including photocopying, recording or by any information storage and retrieval system, without permission from the Publisher in writing.

Typeset in 11/14 Palatino by SJmagic DESIGN SERVICES, India.

Printed and bound by Printworks Global Ltd, London/Hong Kong.

Pen & Sword Books Ltd incorporates the imprints of Pen & Sword Books Archaeology, Atlas, Aviation, Battleground, Discovery, Family History, History, Maritime, Military, Naval, Politics, Railways, Select, Transport, True Crime, Fiction, Frontline Books, Leo Cooper, Praetorian Press, Seaforth Publishing, Wharncliffe and White Owl.

For a complete list of Pen & Sword titles please contact

PEN & SWORD BOOKS LIMITED
47 Church Street, Barnsley, South Yorkshire, S70 2AS, England
E-mail: enquiries@pen-and-sword.co.uk
Website: www.pen-and-sword.co.uk

or

PEN AND SWORD BOOKS
1950 Lawrence Rd, Havertown, PA 19083, USA
E-mail: Uspen-and-sword@casematepublishers.com
Website: www.penandswordbooks.com

CONTENTS

Foreword   6

Chapter 1   Spring   8

Chapter 2   Summer   88

Chapter 3   Autumn   128

Chapter 4   Winter   176

Chapter 5   Finale   215

Bibliography   216

FOREWORD

Inevitably as we travel we see the intertwining of landscape and season. The stark bare knitting of a winter's tree branches provides a fine canopy for the photographer framing a passing modern train. The cold, still air of a frosty morning sets a scene for enhancing spectacular plumes of steam ascending from the hissing locomotive as it departs from a preservation railway station or leaves a lengthy trail of steam and smoke en route through the winter landscape. Snow adds a spectacular special dimension with its blanket reflecting a dazzling sparkle of purest white against a clear, crisp, blue sky. It transforms any landscape so completely with its refined beauty and all-encompassing magnificence. Capturing trains in the snow on camera is ever-captivating, and railway magazines reflect this within their pictorial content found in their publications for many weeks following a significant snowfall.

Springtime's blossom and vivid greens indicating revival and new life always adds a variety of colour to our countryside – and

Calstock Viaduct viewed from the south-east, Saturday 6 November 2010.

a welcome warmth after the cold of winter's sojourn. The vivid light offers new opportunities for a glint off either a modern diesel unit or shining black steam locomotive. Remaining snows atop mountains and moors gleam all the more brightly, providing extra dimension to trains passing through their valleys, contrasted with the opening buds and petals of primroses and daffodils that grace the cuttings of rural branch lines. Later spring's rich rainbow of colours embellishes characteristic station gardens and floral displays which compete for attention alongside the passing trains.

Summer's heat and bright light may not be the photographer's friend but the seasonal increase in seaside specials and visiting locomotives to preserved railways always contributes an interesting dimension – as does the image of trains along coastlines and past tranquil meadows. Mainline steam excursions are usually a more frequent feature, enabling increased opportunities to capture these 'on film'. That extra gradual lengthening of shadow or glow of fading sunlight during the longer evenings provides opportunities for photographing trains that only run this late because of available light.

Autumn always provides a spectacle of red, gold and yellow. Some years are more spectacular than others dependent on preceding dry, cool nights – and railway landscapes are embellished with the display from surrounding trees' fallen leaves and embankment ferns which abundantly bestow their ever-changing golden hues. It's a short but evocative season, all too quickly past, and a tribute to nature's seasonal magnificence.

It could also be argued that the railway has its own changes of season. On the modern railway, traction variety has its own seasons with the passing of the old generation of diesels and electric locomotives and units swiftly replaced by gleaming new types, all seeking the attention of photographers capturing them in favoured locations. What a difference there is to be discovered between a basic 'Pacer' and a new Northern Rail 'Civity' Class 195 diesel unit or between a traditional East Coast High Speed Train and an 'Azuma'! Preserved railways similarly host visiting locomotives on loan, and acquire and transfer their own fleets of locomotives as needs change. The onward tread of progress sees modern electric signalling replacing still extant traditional semaphores – a few last bastions remain – and rural gated level crossings finally replaced by automatic barriers.

One certainty is that the railway landscape, like our own lives, sees seasons of change and it is for us to embrace that which is best represented by each season – the camera captures each scene, the photographer provides the reminiscence and the memory to sustain its timeless value.

I have generally arranged the photographs in this book by the seasons as defined by the astronomical calendar rather than the meteorological calendar, though with one exception when heavy snow had fallen just before the change from autumn to winter. The natural rotation of the Earth around the sun forms the basis for the astronomical calendar, in which we define seasons with two solstices and two equinoxes. To me it best fits the changes we see in nature as the seasons progress. As you patiently travel through each season, so you will share this awe and constant source of inspiration from nature's kaleidoscope of colour. Photographs are in date sequence except where a location is shared by different visit dates in one season, in which case they are also grouped by that location.

The majority of the photographs are digital except where the photograph was taken before acquisition of my first digital camera – a Canon EOS350D – in which case the quality is dictated by how well the negative has kept and the quality of the camera taking the image. Where an unusually rare scene is included, a compromise will have been reached between historicity and best quality available through the tools of Photoshop!

My thanks to my wife Valerie for her always valued helpful support and suggestions, and to Gareth Harrison for acting as a patient and ever ready photographic consultant.

Chapter 1
SPRING

Opposite: Dawlish Sea Wall, Monday 23 March 2020: GB Railfreight Class 50 50007 *Hercules* with one Great Western Mk 3 carriage and an HST power car 43091 tailed by GB Railfreight Class 50 50049 *Defiance* at the rear, forming the 09.16 Long Marston to Laira Depot, both intermediate vehicles having been stored at Long Marston awaiting refurbishment.

   Photographed on the day prior to the first COVID-19 virus lockdown, all looks peaceful although any sense of normality was about to change substantially, and for much longer than anyone could have expected. Also soon to change, also considerably, was the very sea wall along which the trains make their journeys to and fro. This was thanks to much needed renovation and redesigning of the sea wall at a cost of £80 million, from Coastguards breakwater to Boat Cove, after the disastrous storm damage of 2014. Such was the perilous state of the railway along the wall that in stormy weather the CrossCountry 'Voyager' diesel units came to a halt as a result of their roof-mounted brake resistors having a tendency to seize up if penetrated by seawater. It was becoming a literal case of having to cancel CrossCountry services west of Exeter whenever a strong onshore wind, especially from the east, combined with high spring tides. Of much interest has been the eight-legged Wavewalker Jack-up barge, the only one to be found in Europe, which has been used to install around 280 piles between Dawlish station and the Coastguard breakwater, and these will form the foundation of the new sea wall.

Below: Sparkwell, Wednesday 25 March 2020: A pair of Great Western Class 802 IET five-car units forming the 16.15 Plymouth to London Paddington.

   The warmer glow of the early spring sunshine always proves a magnet for drawing people to the countryside. For the author, this involves cycling up a 1 in 5 gradient when ascending the lane that climbs up Hemerdon! Numbers of passengers travelling at this early stage of the COVID-19 virus lockdown were much depressed, although trains were not entirely empty. A regular service was maintained within Devon and also through services to London Paddington. Train lengths were enhanced in order to provide improved safety for 'social distancing' although the Penzance to London services are usually formed of two sets of Class 802 IETs (bi-mode and electric trains) from Plymouth onwards.

Devonport, Monday 26 March 2007: LMS Class 5MT 4-6-0 45407 hauls Past-Time Railtours 'The Harbour Master' 13.42 Plymouth to St Blazey section of the tour to Par Harbour, St Blazey, Par and Newquay.

The cutting at Devonport provides an excellent acoustic studio for recording the echoing sounds of passing steam locomotives as they accelerate away from Plymouth while ascending the 1 in 59 gradient before being immersed in the short Devonport tunnel. The bright sun and darker shadows accentuate the arrival of spring while the white steam contrasts with the black livery worn by the locomotive, further contributing to the scene's atmosphere. The name of the tour is a tribute to the harbours masters of Fowey, Newquay and Plymouth. Their important role is to oversee the safety of navigation for any vessel utilising the port and its approaches. Harbour masters regulate the manner in which vessels conduct their navigation in port.

Worcester Shrub Hill, Wednesday 27 March 2019: Turbostar Class 172 172219 departs with a mid-afternoon service from Great Malvern to Dorridge via Birmingham Snow Hill, passing the fine set of semaphore signals at the north end of the station.

The London Midland livery certainly enhances the sleek appearance of these smart modern diesel units which provide a very comfortable ride. Locations with significant numbers of semaphore signals are increasingly rare; they recall an earlier era when railways retained many complex junctions that have since been replaced by simplified layouts and where speed was sufficiently low to stop at a signal set at horizontal. The signals themselves are the lineside pieces of equipment that indicate to train drivers when it is safe to proceed and what route their train will take. Lineside electric signals permit increased use of the 'four aspect' options of amber and double amber alongside red and green, essential for catering for the longer stopping distances needed by fast-moving express trains. Even these are now becoming outdated in the modern era of cab signalling. Sophisticated computerised and automatic train control systems are far removed from the traditional semaphores which were an everyday furnishing of the steam railway, and the period of transition to diesel and electric accompanied the steady reduction in use of semaphores. It's a part of railway history which is sometimes overlooked and yet a crucial element of the changing nature of this integral aspect of railway operations.

Silverton, Sunday 30 March 2021: Class 802 IET passes at speed with the 15.38 Exeter St Davids to London Paddington.

On the right there appears to have been significant chopping back of lineside trees, which helps open up this view to the north and no doubt also keeps the leaf mulch from autumnal trees creating difficult railhead conditions later in the year. Meanwhile in this welcome springtime warmth and sunlight, the trees are just starting to bud. These impressive Class 800, 801 and 802 bi-mode units are now in service with Great Western Railway, London North Eastern Railway, First TransPennine (as Nova 1) and Hull Trains. Apart from a few glitches with the software for the Great Western five-car Class 802 units and the issue of a lack of seat comfort on the Great Western sets, along with some problems of pantographs tangling with the overhead wires on the East Coast Main Line, they seem to have bedded in very well and are providing improved timings and reliability for each of these operators. Rather amusingly, one of the glitches on the Great Western sets referred to was experienced by the author when two units had been joined up at Plymouth for the onward journey to London. The digital display indicated that the train's next stop was Lipson Junction, followed by Laira Washing Plant – not quite as expected, and an interesting diversion for passengers on board, especially any rail enthusiasts wishing to travel on tracks previously unexplored – although it was eventually rectified by the driver.

As seen from the train window to the right when facing in the direction of travel, there is no evidence that here there were once several sidings which served Silverton Paper Mill to the east of the main line, via a junction off the down main line. They were transfer sidings and engines were not allowed over the paper mill line. A tractor with a buffer plank was used latterly to haul the freight wagons. The siding was taken out of use in August 1967. However, the weighbridge and associated hut, with some rails, are still in situ. *Thanks to Amyas Crump for these details.*

Royal Albert Bridge, Friday 2 April 2021: Viewed from near Antony House (National Trust), Cornwall.
Early springtime foliage is starting to appear on the bushes while the barren branches of the trees starkly await their time for budding to join in the chorus of colour that will soon adorn the Cornish countryside. Brunel's Royal Albert Bridge is revealed unobtrusively as centre guest of this rich tapestry of countryside, estuarial river (the Tamar) and Dartmoor in the background. Along with the shadows and sunlight, they conspire to reach out towards the famous landmark linking Devon and Cornwall, raising their own tribute to this majestic feat of engineering.

Sparkwell, Sunday 4 April 2021: Great Western Class 802 nine-car IET passes with the 10.18 Penzance to London Paddington.

Flowering primroses and gorse growing along the bankside of the Devon main line are bathed in the welcoming warm sunshine of early springtime, and add a splash of colour to the complimentary green livery of this lengthy train as it threads its way towards Cornwood and Blachford viaducts just around the corner. There is an accompanying release from the severe travel restrictions of the recent 'lockdown', imposed as a safety measure to contain COVID-19, and many of the passengers on board may be taking their first long-awaited trip to visit distant family or friends. How many passengers are on board depends on their attitude to risk, and what accommodation requirements they will need at their destinations. Some may be taking the opportunity to travel for its own sake, escaping the confines of their homes and seeking to explore a nearby coastline or countryside walk. This would usually have been a very busy Easter weekend for the many visitors to the South West region but restrictions on accommodation and shop closures remain in place. These trains will gradually become busier as further lockdown measures are lifted. Spring is a season of new life emerging after the depths of winter – and at the time of writing it was hoped that same emergence from restrictions on many of life's opportunities would become a safe release indeed.

Sparkwell, Sunday 4 April 2021: A pair of Class 37s with, front, 37667 in BR green livery and second 37688 in Trainload Construction livery pass with the 'West Wales and West of England' Locomotive Services Limited (LSL) private charter train from Bristol East Yard to Penzance.

It is always interesting to welcome to the South West such visiting trains as this one, especially with their heritage liveries and interesting coaching stock. Spring sunshine and clear air rewards these passengers with scenic views of the surrounding countryside through which they travel.

Compared to many of our European neighbours, the railway scene in the UK is especially colourful, with its diversity in livery usually dictated by the companies in charge of running the services within their allocated franchise areas. Additionally, some operators are willing to allow embellishments and 'heritage' variants to their normal livery, such as happened with the last days of the HSTs on the Great Western and London North Eastern Railway. It can prove a bit of a potpourri but at least it offers a variety to those photographing the usual service trains as well as the charters. It would be an interesting exercise to explore how much attention the wider public gives to such differences. The author had a recent conversation with a casual observer of trains and yet this person always looked out for the nameplates carried by the trains passing his locality. Clearly these details do indeed add a recognisable character and identity to our railways.

Toddington, Gloucestershire and Warwickshire Railway, Saturday 5 April 2008: Class 24 24081, preserved at Gloucestershire and Warwickshire Railway, operating the 14.38 ballast wagons from Winchcombe to Toddington.

This locomotive was restored and returned to service in November 2007. Of interest is the Southern Region brake van immediately behind the locomotive, the iconic 25-ton 'Queen Mary' brake van which was introduced by the Southern Railway in 1936. As these bogie vans were much larger than the usual types, they quickly gained the 'Queen Mary' nickname. Following the steady decline in goods traffic, most of them found further use in departmental service. Brake vans are rather an overlooked reminder of the age of unfitted freights which required the guard's intervention, especially when such trains ascended or descended gradients, or when collecting or dropping wagons at the many railway yards that formed part of the railway infrastructure.

Guards working freight trains would ensure that they had a warming fire, stranded at the far end of the train as necessity dictated, and woe betide the guard who let the fire go out or forgot to light one when starting their shift. It was an unglamorous and thankless yet essential role, often requiring antisocial hours, working during the night. Sometimes guards found themselves working routes traversing fine scenery such as the Settle and Carlisle Railway, and this certainly provided just reward for their mundane duties.

Toddington, Gloucestershire and Warwickshire Railway, Saturday 5 April 2008: Front, Class 37 37215; second, Class 37 37/3 37324, both preserved at the Gloucestershire and Warwickshire Railway, arriving with the 15.10 Cheltenham to Toddington.

It may be a cool spring day but the sunshine helps to highlight the contrasting liveries on each of the Class 37 locomotives, and the young man looking out of the door window with a camera held ready is clearly appreciative of their presence at the head of his train. BR blue has become established as a livery to be admired, even if retrospectively – for there was a time when every diesel and electric was to be painted blue without exception, by order! Pairs of Class 37 locomotives were more likely to be seen on heavy Welsh coal trains than on passenger workings, but preservation allows us to venture beyond the realms of tradition and the sound of both working in tandem will certainly appeal to those travelling in the leading coach, no doubt with its windows wide open and providing a refreshing chill for the other passengers sharing the carriage.

Above: Birkenhead North, Sunday 6 April 1986: Preserved Class 502 electric multiple units M29896 and M28361 preserved by NRM and on loan to Southport Steamport, seen providing short runs to and from Hoylake as part of the Mersey Railway Centenary.

Strictly speaking, Class 503s were the preserve of the Wirral lines, while Class 502s belonged to the Merseyrail Northern Lines emanating from Liverpool Central, and neither strayed to the other's local network. The replacement class 507s and 508s however did form a common pool. This thoughtful gesture to enthusiasts was very much appreciated in providing an opportunity to find one of these units in active use as part of the Mersey Railway Centenary celebrations. In fact, finding preserved electric multiple units running on any part of the electrified sections of the British Railways network is very rare. The LMS maroon looks splendid, unspoilt by any yellow warning panels that would form part of British Railway's stipulated livery requirements for driving cabs. The destination blind's 'Liverpool Express' for the author recalls a short time when Class 502 units formed up direction express trains which ran intermittently between stopping trains from Southport to Liverpool (and also similarly for down trains), calling only at principal stations and passing through small stations, such as at Hightown, with impressive speed.

Opposite: Coombe by Saltash Viaduct, Tuesday 6 April 2021: Class 37 37667 in BR green livery heads the 'West Wales and West of England' Locomotive Services Limited (LSL) private charter train 09.01 from Truro to Plymouth.

Passengers on board this eastbound train can share the view over the River Tamar, caught in luminous spring sunshine, with the lucky residents whose houses border the water, and also with the numerous seagulls looking for fishy elevenses! The Cornish side of the river catches the morning sun although the warmth of such is somewhat compromised at this time of year by the temperature of the tidal water – which is nice and cool. Located just south of Saltash station, the view is especially welcome to those travelling into Cornwall from great distances and who have made the long journey down to the peninsula, as it marks the fact that they have finally arrived in Cornwall. Passports will only be needed on the return to 'England'!

Forder Viaduct, Friday 9 April 2021: Colas Class 67 67027 leading top and tail with 67023, with the 06.08 Reading Triangle to Paignton via Penzance New Measurement Train (NMT).

Spring tides are often noted as causing particularly high sea levels along coasts – with subsequent flooding as sometimes occurs in Looe. 'Neap tides' are those which are lower than average with resultant very low water at low tide, as seen here. When there is a low tide, the Moon faces the Earth at a right angle to the sun so the gravitational force of the moon and sun work against each other. A neap tide happens between two spring tides and occurs twice a month when the first and last quarter Moon appears.

The NMT diagrammed for the West Country monthly trip is more often the specially adapted HST – in full yellow regalia – but on occasions, as also seen in the photograph at Coombe by Saltash Viaduct during a separate visit, it sees these two Class 67s, owned by Network Rail, providing the power. As they pass, the boats await the incoming tide with which they will also rise, and maybe their owners will take advantage of the superb clear spring light and venture out on to the Lynher river estuary, even if clad in warm thermal clothing.

St Denys, Saturday 11 April 1987: Class 33 33004 with Class 73 73101 *Brighton Evening Argus* on a northbound parcels train.

Interestingly the author had haulage behind 73101 on the following Monday, 13 April 1987, on the 09.00 ex-Bournemouth service to London Waterloo as far as Winchester. This was at the time when the Class 73 locomotives were hauling 4TC stock on the Bournemouth 'fasts' for a short while and provided a relatively rare opportunity such for passenger haulage. Whether this train regularly attracted a pair of locomotives I have yet to discover, but the Class 73 may be there for insurance although Class 33s were reliable and more than up to the job for this length of working, even with a steady gradient ahead. More likely is the possibility that the locomotive is merely being moved for a later return passenger working.

St Denys, Saturday 11 April 1987: Class 73 73139 with 2 x 4TC Bournemouth to Waterloo semi-fast service, though it may have been a relief as this was a busy 'Network South East' special day.

The appearance of Class 73 locomotives on passenger workings between the Hampshire coast and London Waterloo during this time was related to when electric motors from Class 432/438 4-REPS were being refurbished for use in 'Wessex Electrics' Class 442s, ready for use in enhanced services provided to the newly electrified Bournemouth to Weymouth line. Five diagrams were provided using pairs of Class 73s initially, but eventually a single Class 73 was proved to be adequate from May 1987. Thus this example looks likely to illustrate a time of transition not only in the use of the Class 73s but also in the reduction from pairing of such locomotives on London 'fast' services.

Winchester, Tuesday 14 April 1987: Class 423 4VEP 7708 passes with the 08.42 London Waterloo to Bournemouth stopping train.

It is a well known saying that today's norm is tomorrow's history, and that applies to transport in particular, as exemplified by the fact that mundane everyday activities of the steam days era now provide acres of photographs in thousands of books recalling such 'halcyon' days, oblivious of the challenges of everyday life that would have faced railway photographers. No doubt I was awaiting to capture on camera something more 'distinctive' than a standard electric multiple unit and yet these formed the basic services with which the 'real' railway operated. Such standard types of traction now form a rare focus in books, usually finely attuned to specific locomotive classes or to distinct regions.

It's a fine spring day and the sunshine raises the interest in the still-new Network SouthEast livery that was so recently introduced in June 1986 to raise the appeal and profile of the many basic commuter trains which were by now receiving their promised new branding and upholstered interiors. This was all thanks to the radical approach taken by visionary managing director Chris Green and which was to revolutionise the concept of rail travel within the commuter belt of the Network SouthEast area of London and the Home Counties.

Winchester, Tuesday 14 April 1987: Class 73 73124 heads north with a civil engineers train, mid-morning.

Here we see a Class 73 locomotive adorned by the large logo version of Intercity livery, and presented in a clean state it looks very smart. Class 73 locomotives were very territorial and rarely strayed from their Southern network area of work. Their dual power mode, with traction current picked up from the third rail and also from the onboard diesel generator set (albeit at reduced power), meant that they were versatile indeed, able to work on both electrified and non-electrified lines. They were rather overshadowed by the more powerful and heavy Type 3 and 4 diesel locomotives in charge of trains elsewhere in Britain, and yet they became an integral part of the Southern railway scene during the 1970s and 1980s when they fulfilled their role with aplomb.

Winchester, Tuesday 14 April 1987: Class 73 73138 in large logo blue livery passes up the rising gradient with a heavy tanker train, mid-morning.

That's quite a load for a small engine, although with 1420hp and maximum rail power of 3150hp to call on while drawing from the third rail supply, it's more than adequate. It is interesting to note that GB Railfreight now owns a fleet of these fifty-year-old locomotives and operates the class in the south-east on various excursion trains, work for Network Rail test-train duties and also hauling Railhead Treatment Trains (RHTTs) and Snow and Ice Treatment Trains (SITTs) to help with clearance during the winter with de-icing vehicles. They generally keep to third rail for such operations but can still use their diesel to operate on non-electrified lines or sidings. Thus the versatility of the class continues to make an impression, and furthermore several heritage railways own examples , often used for civil engineering and maintenance work on their lines.

St Germans Viaduct, Wednesday 15 April 2020: Great Western 'Castle' HST set crosses with the 12.19 Plymouth to Penzance.

Bathed in spring sunshine, the 'Castle' four-car sets have provided a much improved quality of ride for passengers who previously endured Class 150 'Sprinter' two-carriage diesel units on the majority of local services along the Cornish main line. They are a sensible adaptation of the full version of the HST, much suited to the lower speeds demanded by the sinuous curves required by the Cornish hills and valleys which bestow the landscape with such beauty, as seen here. Some are named after local historic sites, helping to establish their revised identity with this region to which they are dedicated. Passengers travelling from Plymouth to western Cornwall previously had to catch an HST originating from London in order to ensure a similar quality of comfort and furthermore, on such services, a buffet service was available – whereas there is no catering on the 'Castle' sets. With a journey time of up to two hours that's a long wait unless you have brought your own drinks and food.

Near Polbathic Bridge, Wednesday 15 April 2020: Great Western 'Castle' HST set climbs out of St Germans with the 13.20 Plymouth to Penzance. The western flank of Dartmoor is visible in the background.

Spring greens abound and contrast with the darker green of Great Western's livery, which in itself pays tribute to the Great Western Railway's trademark green carried by the majority of its steam locomotives. Some enthusiasts and photographers find it less 'adventurous' than liveries applied to main line trainsets belonging to other companies in the privatised sector, for example that of the London North Eastern Railway. It's all a matter of taste, though this author finds the Great Western green to be less eye-catching and more likely to blend in with rural landscapes. The previous FirstGroup's 'Dynamic Lines' livery certainly provided more of a variety of colour in such circumstances.

Above: St Germans Viaduct, Wednesday 15 April 2020: Tidal estuary and piers from south perspective.

The River Tiddy, which flows into the Lynher River is crossed by this awesome viaduct as it passes close to the quiet, characteristic Cornish village of St Germans with its twelfth-century priory church built by the Normans on the site of the old cathedral. It was built in 1908 and is graced with thirteen arches, topped by a granite string course with a brick parapet. Close by the station can be found two truly historic Victorian coaches, each providing self-catering accommodation. One was previously a luggage van with a wood-burning stove and the other a genuine ex-Travelling Post Office (TPO) carriage with clerestory windows stretching its full length. Occasionally, when the author is passing by, a cup of tea seems to be on the brew as guests watch the variety of trains go by from the veranda provided. Fortunately the only trains likely to disturb their overnight slumbers are the night sleeper trains to and from London Paddington, unless they choose a week when engineering trains pass by en route to their work site further down the line.

Opposite: Pitlochry, Sunday 17 April 2011: East Coast Railways HST, with power car 43290 leading, approaches with the 09.40 Inverness to London King's Cross.

Gentle late morning springtime sunshine and shadows greet this long distance train which is seen passing the 1911-built signal box which replaced the 1882 original, and was finally closed in 2019. Evident on the right is the spur of the siding previously serving the goods yard, by this time merely a permanent way siding and looking somewhat disused. Intriguingly, few may have anticipated at this time that within a decade, ex-Great Western four-car short HST sets now operated by ScotRail would be regularly and reliably plying this route between Inverness, Glasgow and Edinburgh.

Dunkeld and Birnam, Sunday 17 April 2011: First ScotRail Class 170/4 170407 in First ScotRail livery, arrives with the 12.30 Inverness to Glasgow Queen Street.

The spring blossom contrasts with the stark branches of the trees awaiting their time of awakening. This diesel unit looks particularly sparkling in the brisk sunlight of early spring, almost as if it has received a recent repaint. The up platform station building, built in 1856 as the terminus of the Perth and Dunkeld Railway, along with the canopy and wall-hung cast iron brackets with their decorative spandrels, exude much character. The distinctive tall octagonal and square-cut ridge chimney stacks are also noteworthy. Dunkeld has a historic road bridge, a fine mediaeval cathedral with characteristic ruins, and scenic walks alongside the River Tay providing a worthwhile visit.

Llangollen, Llangollen Railway, Saturday 18 April 2009: LMS Class 5MT 4-6-0 44806 departs with the 09.30 freight for Carrog.

Now that most freight trains are formed of specialist wagons for moving commodities such as heavy stone, containers, timber or cement, short freights formed of a few wagons and a brake van such as seen here are left to the preservation scene to recreate. They always add an extra dimension of authenticity to special events and are a very welcome addition to photographers' collections. The trail of steam on this cool spring morning helps to enhance the atmosphere as the driver pulls away with a very clean engine – but perhaps that's the giveaway: that this photograph was taken in the context of preservation rather than the true steam era with all its abundant dirt and grime.

Above: Approaching River Dee Viaduct, Llangollen Railway, Saturday 18 April 2009: LMS 'Royal Scot' Class 7P 4-6-0 46100 *Royal Scot* with the 10.00 Llangollen to Carrog express.

With style and grace, this hissing mighty beast strains with all its steam-bathed sinews to haul its train away from the confines of the surrounding Welsh hills, with a sound carried in the still air which echoes to the thrall of all who gaze on such a spectacle. It is intriguing to recall that the design of these powerful locomotives, while purely LMS, was influenced by the GWR 'Castle' class locomotives with their 4-6-0 wheel arrangement (one of which was loaned for trials) and their design followed a set of drawings of the Southern Railway's 'Lord Nelson' class, also 4-6-0s. From late 1931, the Royal Scots carried smoke deflectors, although their use on top expresses was for a relatively short time, as Pacifics replaced them on such duties within ten years. The Midland Railway maroon livery simply enhances the impression conveyed by this magnificent survivor from the golden days of steam-hauled trains.

Opposite above: Glyndyfrdwy, Llangollen Railway, Saturday 18 April 2009: LMS 'Royal Scot' class 7P 4-6-0 46100 *Royal Scot* runs alongside the River Dee with the 14.20 Carrog to Llangollen.

These impressive locomotives were much needed for express work on West Coast Main Line and Anglo-Scottish expresses. When given the distinguished duties of hauling the 'Royal Scot' and 'Midday Scot' trains, they could frequently find themselves in charge of fourteen- or fifteen-carriage loads, which would certainly have provided some heavy weight (of 400–500t) as they clambered up the gradients posed by Shap and Beattock. Pottering alongside the river without any gradient to cause anxiety, it is understandable that there is excess steam to spare and the crew can take a break before their return journey with its demanding climb.

Below: Between Glyndyfrdwy and Carrog, Llangollen Railway, Saturday 18 April 2009: LNER B1 class 4-6-0 1306 *Mayflower* hauls the 15.30 Llangollen to Carrog freight.

The warm spring sunshine gently revives the picturesque rolling landscape where the Welsh hills overlook the River Dee, with the yellow gorse adding a welcome flourish of colour to the multitude of greens. Here is one of the two surviving B1 class locomotives which, in preservation, looks resplendent in its LNER apple green livery, clearly numbered 1306 and named *Mayflower*, although it was only in preservation that the engine had carried any of these features. No. 1306 was built in 1948 by the North British Locomotive Company in Glasgow but was delivered post-nationalisation and carried the number 61306 as bestowed by British Railways. The B1s were designed as mixed traffic locomotives capable of hauling express passenger trains as well as freight traffic. They were powerful engines which worked across many railway routes from East Anglia to Scotland, including the Great Central Railway.

Between Glyndyfrdwy and Carrog, Llangollen Railway, Saturday 18 April 2009: LMS Class 5MT 4-6-0 44806 hauls the 16.12 Carrog to Llangollen alongside the River Dee. At the rear is GWR 'Dukedog' 3200 class 4-4-0 9017, in 1950's BR plain black. Note the 'Beavertail' observation car 1719E forming the rear carriage.

The 'Dukedog' locomotive would have been most at home on this railway, as also on any of the ex-Cambrian lines west of Shrewsbury. The Cambrian main line was lightly built, and permanent way restrictions forbade the use of heavier locomotives. This meant that only a few classes of GWR locomotive were allowed to run over it. As a result, the 'Duke' class locomotives were given a life extension after they were becoming uneconomical to repair. These became known as 'Dukedogs', for they were rebuilt using spare 'Duke' class boilers. Passengers travelling in the observation car will have a fine view of this hybrid, though they will need to be prepared to waive the fact that they are travelling in a carriage built for the LNER at Doncaster in 1937 for the 'Coronation' high speed train services between London and Edinburgh and more associated with being behind a Class A4 for their trusty steed!

Silverton, Sunday 18 April 2021: Colas Class 70 70808 hauls track panels for the Okehampton line engineering upgrade associated with its forthcoming two-hourly weekday passenger service.

The old Silverton station house enjoys a grandstand view of the Great Western mainline in this part of East Devon. Not that Sunday engineering trains feature prominently in its usual traffic passing by, but this one must provide the necessary materials for the heavy work to be undertaken in the week ahead. Indeed, the previous train an hour or so earlier had been a Colas Class 56 also with a similarly associated engineering train, so the owner may have been poised with a pen to record the passing visiting tractions' numbers, if so inclined. A frequent diagram for trains bringing down all the various materials needed by the civil engineer from around early March meant that the owner could be set for quite a busy time assuming they have a modicum of interest in the increased variety of trains passing their front door.

Above and below: Glenfinnan Viaduct, Tuesday 19 April 2011: View with Beinn an Tuim the nearest prominent mountain in background.

Beinn an Tuim's awesome height (2,657ft, 810m) certainly dominates the scene of this famed viaduct which carries the single track West Highland Railway (Mallaig extension) over the valley of the River Finnan. Constructed by Robert McAlpine & Sons, it was built from mass concrete – such innovative use of concrete on this scale was an industry first. The viaduct affords magnificent views over Loch Shiel and the Glenfinnan monument, built in 1815 as a poignant reminder of the clansmen who gave their lives to the Jacobite cause in the 1745 Jacobite Rising. Steam-hauled 'Jacobite' trains as well as the regular timetabled DMUs slow when crossing to allow passengers to absorb the unsurpassed vista of the West Highlands. Given favourable weather conditions such as here, the impressive landscape really is breathtaking and the photographer was indeed very fortunate to capture the location in such clear light. Admittedly most of the passengers on board will opt to take in the view over the Loch rather than that of the glowering mountain behind them. The bleached grass of the mountainside reminds us that this is still spring and the grass has yet to be revitalised by necessary warmth. Those who engineered the line could hardly have expected the global fame acquired by this viaduct in association with a certain magician …

Above and below: Loch Awe Side Viaduct, Thursday 21 April 2011: ScotRail Class 156/4 units cross the River Orchy with the 08.21 Glasgow Queen Street to Oban followed by the 12.11 Oban to Glasgow Queen Street. Centre: Beinn á Chochuill, height 980m (3220ft); right: Beinn Eunaich height 988m (3245ft).

   Here we must let the mountain scenery exude its magnificence even if the passing trains appear somewhat daunted! The snows of winter have melted leaving the babbling brooks and gushing waterfalls to meet the pure waters of the flowing river. Serene and silent, the splendour of the Scottish mountains standing sentry to ages past is unsurpassed in this springtime clear air, shared only by those courageous enough to climb their peaks and by solitary fishermen knee-deep in the valley river waters patiently awaiting that pike or salmon to take the bait. The River Orchy flows into nearby Loch Awe, the longest lake in Scotland, and it is certainly an impressive railway viaduct which crosses at this point. The local climate at the loch is surprisingly benign so close to the surrounding mountains and the author has advice based on reliable local knowledge that winter snow at the lowest level is infrequent. The mountains tell a different story, of course. One wonders if any driver of these trains through the changing seasons along this route can tire of its spectacular landscapes.

Hemerdon Bank, Sunday 21 April 1991: Class 50 50027 *Lion* crests the summit on a mid-afternoon eastbound empty coaching stock (ECS) movement.

It looks like this train is about to enter Hemerdon loop, according to the signal aspect displayed, indicating that the points are set for such. The Class 50 is not therefore accelerating hard at speed, as may be suggested by the exhaust being emitted, otherwise it would certainly derail. More likely it has just completed ascending Hemerdon's steep gradient and is still needing power in order to divert into the loop. Presumably an up express is scheduled to pass. The Network SouthEast livery worn by both locomotive and carriages proved an attraction to photographers, especially when it reached parts of the rail network lying beyond Network SouthEast boundaries – which Plymouth certainly was, Exeter St Davids being the official western limit as served by trains from London Waterloo. No. 50027 was officially withdrawn on 23 July 1991 after a career spanning twenty-three years and is preserved at the Mid-Hants Railway in working order.

Liverpool Lime St, Thursday 23 April 1987: Class 31 31425, 10.45 to Yarmouth. Class 142 'Pacer' for Preston on the right.

This train operated during the winter timetable on weekdays and brought Class 31s to the Liverpool area at a time when they were still, in their everyday use, very territorial to the Eastern Region. Admittedly the train only has to reach Sheffield in order to achieve such metals. The purpose of providing such a train in the timetable is intriguing. It wasn't that thousands of folk from the north-west would choose to travel all the way to its destination when there were a multitude of coastal resorts along the Lancashire and North Wales coasts so much nearer. My own experience of these locomotives was generally on the Birmingham to Leicester route where I visited a friend who lived at the latter. He once drove to Narborough to collect me from that station only for me to see him with an astonished look on his face as I flew past at great speed, head out of the carriage window enjoying the sound of the adjacent locomotive but overlooking that I had misread the timetable – and its next stop was Leicester! Fortunately he swiftly resolved any dilemma by meeting me at Leicester's station foyer.

Stretchford, South Devon Railway, Sunday 24 April 2011: Class 25 D7612 25262 hauls the 15.57 Totnes to Buckfastleigh.

Emerging from the shadows into the late April sunshine, the Class 25 here appears to embrace the warmth that it encounters, and its passengers will almost certainly share that welcome. This locomotive has supplied reliable service during the summer season of 2021 on the South Devon Railway hauling strengthened trains facilitating social distancing. It has been rostered for the last diagram of most weekdays, and has drawn many admirers for its characteristic rasping Sulzer sound echoing off the river banks as it passes by in the evening light. The author has acted as guard on some of these trains, and the locomotive has certainly provided an invigorating ride.

Royal Albert Bridge, Sunday 25 April 2004: EWS Class 67 67020 crosses with a VSOE excursion from Par to Exeter, early afternoon.

Luxury trains such as this provide a very high quality 'taster' type of travel experience amidst fine scenery, and the Pullman livery applied to the carriages adds an extra appeal. White tablecloths, waiter service and champagne breakfasts, or delicious lunches and afternoon teas, coddle the lucky passengers on board. It all recalls an era when to travel was perceived as just as important as to arrive at the destination, and prior to onboard catering, stops would be made by long-distance trains at important stations en route where refreshment rooms provided nourishing meals and there were plenty of people ready to meet and feed the hungry passengers – quite a logistics exercise! Even in recent times the author recalls an announcement by the catering manager on board the up late afternoon Great Western Plymouth to London Paddington HST advertising half-lobster as being available to those taking dinner in the buffet car – and the breakfasts served on the 06.00 up London service were always very popular, being considered a highlight by businessmen travelling for meetings in the capital.

Golant, Saturday 26 April 1986: Plymouth Railway Circle 'Class 118 Farewell Tour' with British Telecom and standard BR blue livery Class 118 DMUs.

Quite what the current health and safety regime would have to say about passengers informally walking alongside the 'six foot' without guard rails on the estuary side of the embankment we must leave to conjecture – but no one got run over or fell into the mud on this occasion. It's still possible to see a similar casual approach to rail safety in some Central European countries but far less with those on the near Continent. This special train saw passengers also disembark at Carbis Wharf, Burngullow and Parkandillick, which the train also visited on this fine spring day. Where such freedom to walk over active lines might be permitted there would now be a sea of distractive fluorescent orange jackets worn by participants who would be carefully shepherded along by an appropriate ratio of officials. The need to complete lengthy off-site Outdoor Educational Activities Planning and Notification Forms by the author for any school student visits and trips reflects the increased attention to such safety issues which necessarily in turn reflects concerns over negligence that may have been previously overlooked. Our modern-day railways' and schools' safety systems ensure a necessarily very high level of protection.

Medstead and Four Marks, Mid-Hants Railway, Saturday 27 April 2002: Front, Class 46 46035 *Ixiom* in BR blue livery; second, Class 20 D8188/20188 in black livery, arrive with an early afternoon service from Alresford to Alton.

The foliage in the trees has yet to flourish and the denuded branches clearly reveal several birds' nests which are no doubt harbouring chicks – who will be oblivious to the interesting rail traffic passing close by during this diesel gala event. Spring is a popular time for steam and diesel galas on preservation railways as it provides the first real opportunity for locomotives and onlookers alike to stretch their legs after the dark and gloomy days of winter, and of course for the railways to boost their coffers. Heavy steam-hauled expresses would have passed this way when diverted off the main line from London to Hampshire and Dorset, especially during the 1950s at weekends during the third-rail electrification of that route. Less likely would have been the appearance of the heavy Class 46 locomotives which held sway over the London Midland division routes. Still, it all looks the part for a location that might easily pass for Derbyshire.

Hemerdon Bank, Sunday 28 April 1991: Class 47/7 47707 *Holyrood* ascends with the 14.55 Plymouth to London Waterloo.

Spring greens are cautiously making an appearance though the trees here, but remain convinced that winter has yet to recede. Many of the fleet of initially Scottish Class 47/7 (47701 to 716) push/pull locomotives were cascaded to Old Oak Common in the late 1980s and early 1990s where some found later employment in the South West with such interesting workings as this through-service from Plymouth to London Waterloo along the Southern route via Salisbury, and they gained the Network SouthEast livery as part of this process. No doubt the Southern Region was happier with these operating the route rather than Class 50s which were considered to hammer the track and cause increased engineering repairs. Certainly the route from Plymouth to Newton Abbot and then from Honiton to Salisbury would provide some hefty gradients for these locomotives to prove themselves, and a journey behind either a Class 47, Class 50 or even Class 33 was certainly bound to provide music to the ears of the rail enthusiasts seeking such haulage through the pleasant undulating countryside that accompanied this route.

Interestingly, the Class 47s had a lower fuel range than the Class 50s and were slower to reach their higher speed than the Class 50s. This hindered their performance on the Exeter to London Waterloo route with its relatively large number of station stops, from each of which they had to accelerate in order to reach the higher speeds demanded by the scheduled timings. Furthermore, they wore through brake blocks very quickly on the hilly route, which posed a problem as the Southern servicing sheds of Eastleigh and Salisbury were not interested in diesels, so replacing the blocks had to be done at Exeter (in the old steam shed!) which, at the far west of the route, was not convenient if the problem developed at the London end.

Newton St Cyres, Thursday 29 April 2021: Colas Class 66/8 66848 leads as it approaches the station with a morning loaded ballast for the Okehampton line engineering upgrade.

  We previously saw the Class 70 at Silverton hauling track panels for this major engineering project in the photograph on page 35. Here we see further evidence of the considerable logistics of moving ballast to the various sites along the Okehampton branch. This train, one of two morning departures from Westbury, was assisted at the rear by Class 66847 and had fifteen heavily loaded wagons to haul up the grade. The countryside around Newton St Cyres consists of gently rolling hills with traditional farms and barns, orchards, fields with abundant crops including cereals and rape seed, and local beehives. The village is not too remote, being only just over 4 miles from the bustling city of Exeter, and yet the author came across a horse and cart trotting through the village centre during this visit! There is a well reputed pub by the station which brews its own beer and can be accessed by train most easily on a Sunday – on other days the traffic is deemed inadequate for more than a very limited service for commuters. It is not unusual to find customers joining Exeter-bound trains on a late Sunday afternoon having imbibed perhaps a little more than is best for them after a relaxing session therein.

Winchcombe, Gloucestershire and Warwickshire Railway, Sunday 30 April 2000: GWR Class 1400 0-4-2T 1450 departs with an afternoon service from Toddington to Gotherington.

There is quite a contrast between the established spring blossom and lush vegetation seen here in Gloucestershire as compared to that seen in Devon in the previous photograph, even though it was taken on almost the same day of the month. Maybe the winter had been less harsh in the millennium year? The bracket signal protects Winchcombe station and is well situated to the east of Greet Tunnel through which this train will shortly traverse. Its journeying along one of the UK's longest preserved railways (at over 14 miles), especially with the section to Broadway now open, though not at the date of this picture. The author visited Toddington, the main location for starting a visit and home to the locomotive shed, in February 1986 when this was merely a fledgling preservation line yet to become established. Now it is a leading attraction providing steam and diesel events and regular themed days drawing such vast crowds that a field adjacent to Toddington station is now to be used to accommodate all the visitors' cars.

Blachford Viaduct, Sunday 5 May 1991: Class 50 50007 *Sir Edward Elgar* hauls the 14.55 Plymouth to London Waterloo.

    This Class 50 was given a special livery of Brunswick green in February 1984, and renamed *Sir Edward Elgar* as part of the celebrations for the 150th anniversary of the Great Western Railway. This proved a very popular choice and it is not far removed from that version of green which now adorns the Great Western IET fleet.

    The sheep graze, oblivious to its passing, unaware of the irony that it will in fact traverse the Southern Railway route to Waterloo rather than take the Berks and Hants Railway that forms the Great Western route to London Paddington. It's worth a thought that in preservation it was repainted in BR blue and recently has been acquired by GBRf in association with the Class 50 Alliance, and painted into that company's livery, as seen in our very first springtime photograph. The Class 50s reliability on the Plymouth/Exeter to London Waterloo services eventually became challenged by issues such as recurrence of flashovers, and this was overcome by a team of dedicated riding inspectors on board the services which were booked for Class 50 haulage. This reassured the drivers who in turn did their best to keep the locomotives going and work as a team with the inspectors to resolve problems as they arose.

Above: Laira Embankment, Plymouth, Friday 7 May 2021: CrossCountry HST with power cars 43301 and 43357 passes with the 12.27 service to Edinburgh.

Stalwart CrossCountry HSTs make a welcome appearance now that the Class 800 IETs have replaced the Great Western fleet, and they certainly ensure a more comfortable ride for all passengers on board but especially those making the long journey to Scotland, for the alternative Voyagers are far inferior in comfort and quality of ride.

The high tide in the River Plym Estuary causes a gentle swell and the warmer sunshine promises later spring's warmth, especially after the previous month of unusually cool and dry weather during 2021. The mottled colours of the moor suggest there is more cloud, giving a chance of a shower to quench the parched fields and upland pastures.

Opposite above: Roebuck Farm, West Somerset Railway, Saturday 11 May 2002: GWR Class 6101 2-6-2T 4160 passes with the 16.55 Minehead to Bishops Lydeard.

This pastoral scene is very typical of springtime in Somerset with its babbling brooks carrying the plentiful water from frequent rain showers over the nearby Quantocks and also the sunlit verdant green grass here providing a contrast to the Great Western green carried by the passing locomotive as it sustains its 1 in 100 gradient climb towards Crowcombe. The marshy ground indicates why an embankment is useful at this point and hints of the local red sandstone are evident in the bridge brick arch. It's a truly idyllic landscape, and the many signed footpaths suggest that walkers and hikers make tracks for this area of outstanding beauty.

The Great Western was more interested in serving the coastal towns of West Somerset – hence the purpose of building the railway from Taunton to Minehead – which means that, apart from the occasional passing train, the local nature here remains undisturbed in this part of Somerset with its tree encompassed, roughly surfaced single track lanes discouraging use by heavy trucks and lorries, caravans and motorised homes which sensibly prefer to keep to the main roads. The exception is the milk lorries wending their way between the farms, and occasions when convoys of railway photographers converge for special timetables and events on the preserved railway!

Below: Roebuck Farm, West Somerset Railway, Saturday 11 May 2002: 'Western' Class 52 D1010 *Western Campaigner* in BR maroon livery passes with the 16.55 Bishops Lydeard to Minehead.

  The pure maroon livery without yellow warning panels is here enhanced by the sandstone in the bridge arch and was considered one of the better liveries to be carried by the 'Western' class diesel hydraulics, perhaps because it so well blended with the sandstone of south Devon's coastline. Even purist steam photographers of the early 1960s were prepared to press their camera shutter button to capture these distinct locomotives, maybe assisted by the impressive drone conveyed by the hum of their Maybach engines. The sleek length of the locomotives also meant that any livery variety applied was bound to be influential to the impression conveyed, and several varieties of livery were carried in due course of time, some uniquely, such as that of 'desert sand'. In that era of otherwise BR green for modern traction, at least for diesels, it was all very welcome and helped keep the Western Region as a clearly defined sector of the UK railway scene.

Bishops Lydeard, West Somerset Railway, Saturday 11 May 2002: Class 33 D6566/33048 in BR blue livery awaits departure with the 19.00 evening return service to Minehead.

The longer evening light available from mid-May is always welcome and scenes that would have been enveloped in darkness during autumn and winter become increasingly available to the photographer. By late September, the light at this time of day will have become increasingly gloomy and it is indeed a relatively short time that the late spring and summer provides to enjoy such benefits. Some preserved railways take advantage of this by providing fish and chip evening specials, or evening dining trains.

The West Somerset Railway operates such an evening dining train, the 'Quantock Belle', which is staffed entirely by volunteers from the West Somerset Railway Association and runs on selected Saturday evenings and Sunday lunchtimes from April to November. This however could well be one of the former, although the author did not, in this case, participate. There is usually a need for a local fish and chip shop to be readily available to supply such quantities as are required at relatively short notice. One can imagine the hurried order for 'Cod and chips times forty please' followed by the essential reply, 'With or without salt and vinegar?' Passengers on board will have the opportunity to enjoy the setting sun over Exmoor and the Bristol Channel while on their journey back to Minehead, with maybe a glimpse of an owl or hawk patrolling the local countryside for their own evening meal.

Blachford Viaduct, Saturday 15 May 2010: Front, GWR 4900 'Hall' class 4-6-0 4965 *Rood Ashton Hall*; second, GWR 4073 'Castle' class 4-6-0 5043 *Earl of Mount Edgcumbe* cross the viaduct with 'The Cornishman' Vintage Trains railtour, 16.30 from Plymouth to Birmingham Snow Hill, behind steam to Bristol Temple Meads.

   The title of *Earl of Mount Edgcumbe* refers to that held in the Peerage of Great Britain. The nameplate of 5043 will have more meaning for those living in the West Devon area. The ancestral seat of the Edgcumbe family is Mount Edgcumbe House, near Plymouth, which is located in spectacular grounds and very popular with visitors who travel over on the Cremyll ferry. The title included the honorary post of Deputy Lord Warden of the Stannaries, from 1913 to 1944. Locally mined tin and copper was brought twice a year, until 1838, for assaying and stamping in the stannary towns of Bodmin, Liskeard, Lostwithiel, Helston and Truro. All tin was coined in each of the stannary towns in the presence of a warden. The technique of assaying involved cutting off a corner of each ingot to assay its tin content. In this way the collection of tin coinage, which was the duty payable on the metal tin, was fulfilled. This permitted those owning the tin mines supplying the stannaries to sell to whom they pleased, once this coinage tax was paid to the crown.

Approaching Staverton, South Devon Railway, Sunday 20 May 2001: Class 20 20118 passes with the 12.32 Totnes to Buckfastleigh.

In the first decade of the twentieth century the South Devon Railway hosted no less than two Class 20 locomotives, although these have since moved on to other sites. Despite their age – well over fifty years old – approximately twenty-five of these locomotives have been preserved, and they are popular with enthusiasts and with those responsible for maintaining the preserved railways on which they are situated. This is partly because of a wider availability of spare parts for when repairs are needed and because their low weight and moderately powered engine means that they are relatively economical to operate – for example, with maintenance trains or during off-peak times when passenger loadings are not too demanding. Their characteristic English Electric engines emit a distinct whistle similar to that of the Class 40 locomotives. Their appearance is also well defined whether viewed from the nose end, as here, or from the end with the cab.

As seen with 20118 the Class 20 locomotives up to D8127 were fitted with disc indicators in the style of the steam era. It was common in BR days to find Class 20s paired together at the nose, with their cabs at opposite ends, ensuring that the driver could quite clearly see the road ahead. This Class 20 in later years saw use with GB Railfreight, still in BR Railfreight grey with red stripe, working on such train as movements of London Transport 'S' stock from Derby to Old Dalby.

Kentsford Farm Crossing, West Somerset Railway, Sunday 21 May 2000: 'Western' Class 52 D1023 *Western Fusilier* hauls the 12.15 Minehead to Bishops Lydeard.

Looking splendid in its pristine BR blue with full yellow front livery, it was fortunate to capture this example of the class in action, its base of preservation being located at the National Railway Museum. In fact, of the seventy-four 'Western' class locomotives that were built, seven are preserved, of which the Diesel and Electric Preservation Group based at Williton on the West Somerset Railway owns D1010 *Western Campaigner*, and this locomotive is the pride of the fleet at Williton. Keeping it in good working order has sometimes proved a trial, but it has made various appearances on the line over the years, usually but not exclusively at the annual spring mixed-traffic gala.

Plymouth Friary Sidings, Saturday 22 May 2004: Class 40 40145 (preserved on the East Lancashire Railway) detaches from carriages having recently arrived with the 07.00 Crewe to Plymouth 'Western Whistler II' operated by Pathfinder Tours in association with the Class 40 Preservation Society.

This was previously London and South Western Railway territory and first saw passenger trains from July 1891 when the goods station at Friary was opened as a passenger terminus. The Friary branch saw such prestigious locomotives as Lightweight Pacifics hauling through trains for London Waterloo and Brighton as well as 'Moguls' hauling more local fare to Exeter Central, or O2s working their gated stock on the branch to Turnchapel.

Springtime growth of weeds and flowers underline the rarity of anything traversing this branch now, and it terminates before the road bridge from which this photograph was taken – a modern shopping complex now occupies the site of the Southern's station terminus (behind the photographer). The name of the excursion here echoes the term of endearment given to the Class 40 locomotives with their distinct whistle.

Carlisle, Monday 25 May 1992: Class 47/4 47580 *County of Essex* in large logo BR blue livery with Traintours' 'Pilkington' excursion coaching set, arriving from Settle and Carlisle route, mid-afternoon.

This Pilkington green, red and blue Mk 1 coaching set that ran in the early 1990s either appealed to or disgusted photographers and passengers alike – but it certainly turned heads. It all depends on what you consider a 'striking' livery. Some European railway operators, especially in Germany, permit advertising to embrace the full locomotive or multiple unit while the hauled coaching stock retains the nationalised colour scheme. Swiss Railways' 'Golden Pass' livery carries photographs of Swiss Alpine scenery to promote both the train and the scenery to onlookers. GB Railfreight's Class 66 66720 earned its bright rainbow livery after the company held a competition for the children of employees to design a locomotive livery. Wessex Trains happily adorned its Class 153 DMUs with half-length photographic features of West Country ports and historic cities. Streamlined horizontal colour stripes seem to be a preference within the UK scene. The final verdict will always be subjective and it can be an emotive subject.

Ryde St John's Road, Isle of Wight, Wednesday 27 May 1992: Class 483 prepares to depart on the 12.10 to Ryde Pier Head, 11.52 ex-Shanklin.

Even the Isle of Wight was not spared the standardised Network SouthEast branding – after all, it is part of the mainland's Southern Railway territory, and quite intentionally so. It all looks very smart on this 1938-built train which had previously operated for London Transport's Underground. Note the down platform start signal with elevated ground rotating disc signals, with the left hand disc signal being for the bay platform. The signal box controls the whole of the Island Line, Brading and Sandown signal boxes having been decommissioned in 1989 – it was previously in use at London Waterloo East!

For those who value such historic railway features, much of the appeal about the island's railway system has been that modernisation had eluded most of its daily operation and this has remained the case until recent times.

Ryde St John's Road, Wednesday 27 May 1992: Class 485 485043 stabled.

This is an even more vintage EMU than seen in the previous photograph, a 1967 BR rebuild of London Transport 1923-25 stock. It reinforces just how modernisation has *not* been the priority for upgrading the fleet of trains used on the Island Line. There is a promise of new Class 484 Vivarail converted ex-London Underground D-Stock two-car trains in the imminent future at the time of writing. However, this investment will cost Network Rail much more than anticipated as the track at Brading will need lowering for the new trains, required for the foot crossing at the Shanklin end of the platforms to meet relevant safety regulations. Platforms at Ryde St Johns will need to be lowered, and those at Esplanade raised to comply with accessibility regulations.

Warmer spring weather often attracts day trips from the mainland to the beaches and towns of the island with a trip across the Solent adding to the appeal of such. Wouldn't it be marvellous if at least some of the branch lines that were closed on the island could be brought back into use, as light rail systems, to combat the increasing problem of overcrowded roads during the busier tourist season from late spring through to late September?

Above: Chorleywood, Saturday 27 May 2000: LNER Class B12 4-6-0 61572 passes with the 'Steam on the Met'.

During the 1990s and in the millennium year, following previous celebrations to commemorate the centenary of the opening of the Metropolitan Railway to Chesham, London Underground ran steam specials from Amersham to Watford and these were promoted as 'Steam on the Met'. Metropolitan Railway electric locomotive no. 12, *Sarah Siddons*, was also employed. These were very popular both with rail enthusiasts and the general public although they were logistically complicated for London Underground as they had to run the steam services in between the normal Metropolitan and Chiltern services. A special set of coaches was used and facilities were provided at Neasden for the steam locomotives. It certainly provided an intriguing spectacle in the Metropolitan Railway's 'Metroland', so epitomised by avenues of mock-Tudor *country* villas and semi-detached dwellings with steep roofs, bay windows and half-timbered gables. Such integration of steam trains within the normal busy service of frequent London Transport trains kept cameras busy at locations where the sight of steam trains in the modern era was most irregular.

Opposite: Llangollen, Llangollen Railway, Saturday 29 May 2004: GWR Class 5101 2-6-2T 5199 in a light engine movement, early afternoon.

Dwarfed by a very tall tree, the locomotive's size seems almost irrelevant and yet the power and weight of these large Prairie locomotives meant that they were kept very busy and could handle gradients with ease. There are several in preservation and they can be entrusted to haul well-loaded trains along such demanding lines as found here and on the West Somerset Railway. No. 5199 will face a gradient of 1 in 80 past Berwyn, once attached to the carriages in the down platform, thus providing superb sound and spectacle for those on board as well as any awaiting photographers taking advantage of lineside locations to capture the spirit of the Great Western in rural Wales.

Above: Llangollen, Llangollen Railway, Saturday 29 May 2004: Class 47/4 47449/D1566 in BR green arrives with the 13.30 from Carrog.

Two-tone British Railways green livery was very admirable when kept clean, though it was prevalent during the days of transition from steam to diesel, and diesel locomotives then shared their stables with steam locomotives in or alongside steam sheds, both of the latter in their increasingly grimy and unkempt condition. It was therefore often the case that they looked less bright and clean than demonstrated here. Being a workhorse for any type of train, Class 47 locomotives would have been at home with most trains requiring faster speeds and therefore they would have seen use on mail and parcels trains constituted by such stock, as seen in the sidings alongside the locomotive shed on the right.

Opposite above: Douglas, Isle of Man Steam Railway, 30 May 1998: 2-4-0T no. 11 *Maitland* shunts coaching stock for a morning departure.

Such vintage locomotives as this Beyer-Peacock 1905-built locomotive with its train of late nineteenth- and early twentieth-century original coaches are all part of the fascinating transport heritage to be found on the railways and tramways of the island. The railway passes through woodland glens and along scenic coastal landscapes, bypassing quaint historic halts full of charm and character, while providing an appealing glimpse of the landscape found in the southern half of the island. The 'Go Explore' tickets allow unlimited travel at remarkable value on most of the heritage transport systems on the island – and includes bus travel which helps access to parts of the island which can't be reached by these. As ever, luck with the weather greatly helps. On my visits over to the island, often in late May, I have enjoyed mostly fine days, often with better weather than that found experienced by the mainland at the same time. However, a word of caution – avoid TT race-time unless you are seriously into motorcycles!

Below: Near Rhyd Ddu, Welsh Highland Railway, Sunday 30 May 2010: NGG16 Class 2-6-2 + 2-6-2T no. 87 ex-South African Railways, seen hauling 10.00 Caernarfon to Beddgelert and Pont Croesor.

This smart looking 1ft 11½in gauge locomotive was built by Cockerill to the Garratt design of its sisters. Towards its journey's end it will be venturing along the very recently reopened (26 May 2010) section of line beyond Beddgelert. The fine spring sunshine highlights the Snowdon range and newly-born lambs graze contentedly on the tasty Welsh grass. The scurrying clouds contribute their own interest to the atmosphere of this scene though the photographer waits ever nervously to see if one intervenes to block out the light just as the train arrives in the camera's viewfinder.

Above: Rhyd Ddu, Welsh Highland Railway, Sunday 30 May 2004: NG G16 Class 2-6-2 + 2-6-2T Beyer Garratt no. 138 *Millennium* arrives with 10.30 from Caernarfon.

The Welsh spring weather looks changeable with threatening clouds hugging the Snowdon range, but these passengers seem to be enjoying themselves and have the benefit of a bright spell as they arrive at what was the railways southern limit at the time of the photograph. Since then the line has been completed all the way to Porthmadog via the scenic splendours of the Aberglaslyn Pass. It's a superb railway in terms of scenery and motive power, with the impressive sound of the hard-working steam locomotives echoing from the surrounding hills and valleys.

Opposite: Rhyd Ddu, Welsh Highland Railway, Sunday 30 May 2004: NG G16 Class 2-6-2 + 2-6-2T Beyer Garratt no. 138 *Millennium* is seen around midday between Snowdon Ranger and Rhyd Ddu, hauling the 12.00 to Caernarfon.

The Snowdon mountain range glowers over the almost insignificant train as it snakes its way around the many tortuous reverse curves at Rhyd Ddu. No standard gauge line could manage such necessary twists and turns and the value of narrow gauge is clearly evident as the train clambers between granite rock outcrops and the mountain slopes. The cooler air enhances the trail of steam as the locomotive crew work hard at feeding the fiercely glowing firebox. All these ingredients combine to keep the railway photographers and on-board passengers enthralled. It is indeed a rewarding tribute to those who had the vision to reinstate the railway and see it reopened as a new marketing opportunity. It has become a successful attraction for the Welsh tourist trade and has also provided a link between the historic town of Caernarfon and the Porthmadog base of the Ffestiniog railway, especially after such a long absence of passengers from as early as 1936.

Opposite above: Near Betws Garmon, Welsh Highland Railway, Sunday 30 May 2004: NG G16 Class 2-6-2 + 2-6-2T Beyer Garratt no. 138 *Millennium* passes with the 13.30 from Caernarfon with a service for Rhyd Ddu.

We see the train passing through the Vale of Betws Garmon as it climbs towards Rhyd Ddu. The wagon provided for cycles is proving its worth with at least three being conveyed, no doubt for some off-road cycling in the hills and woodland ahead. The Alfred County Railway overhauled this locomotive when it was in South Africa and converted it to oil firing – a characteristic of the black clag emitted from the chimney, although later (after this photograph was taken) it was converted back to coal firing during 2012.

Opposite below: Rhyd Ddu, Welsh Highland Railway, Sunday 30 May 2004: NG G16 Class 2-6-2 + 2-6-2T Beyer Garratt no. 143 arrives with the 15.00 from Caernarfon.

The impressive size of the railway's Beyer-Garratt built locomotives is reinforced by their 62-ton weight, and they certainly hold their presence even when surrounded by the daunting mountains that form the Snowdon range. Truly giants in their realm of narrow gauge railways, the Beyer-Garratts are just as impressive as their larger brothers built for South African Railways as Class GMA, typically evidenced by Beyer Garratt no. 4112 (3ft 6in gauge) weighing in at 156t. The latter arrived in the UK for preservation still in operating condition and was initially to be seen at the Plym Valley Railway with all of its works plates and manufacture details intact, partly in Afrikaans.

Betws Garmon, Welsh Highland Railway, Sunday 30 May 2004: NG G16 class 2-6-2 + 2-6-2T Beyer Garratt no. 138 *Millennium* passes with the 15.00 from Rhyd Ddu to Caernarfon.

Here the railway crosses the Afon Gwyrfai, and we find a variety of spring greens intruding (with abundance) with which the metallic light green livery blends well. The fireman keeps a wary eye as the locomotive exerts its weight as it traverses the bridge. It's really a green goddess in disguise! Steam exudes from its many pores accompanied by a light hissing rather than the heavy blast that would have been heard during the locomotive's ascent.

Waunfawr, Welsh Highland Railway, Sunday 30 May 2004: NG G16 class 2-6-2 + 2-6-2T Beyer Garratt no. 138 *Millennium* arrives with the 18.00 from Rhyd Ddu with a service for Caernarfon.

Late spring evenings offer the advantage of photography, which is always especially appreciated as sunset becomes later by the day – in total contrast to the darkness of long winter nights. Passengers can enjoy a full day's light for a lengthy day out on the railway and walkers can return later after a longer walk. Timetables can permit later running of services though no doubt the crew on board the locomotive will be looking forward to arrival at the destination before they carry out their final duties, which will probably include filling the boiler with water for the following day, running the fire irons through the fire to deaden or 'kill' the fire, and break up any clinker from the fire bars. Clinker is the remnants of the coal and sets like concrete on the fire bars, starving them of air. The smokebox at the front of the engine must be opened and ash shovelled out, either onto a collection area or maybe into a wheelbarrow.

Ansty, Oxford Canal, Sunday 30 May 2021: Avanti West Coast Pendolino Class 390 390132 passes with 13.35 Manchester Piccadilly to London Euston.

Late spring brings fine warm days which draw out the narrowboats onto the many canals that interlink the towns and cities of the Midlands and North of England in particular. Many are meticulously presented in a sheen of glossy green or blue paint while others reveal a more workaday facade indicating that their owner is probably less interested in the tourist narrowboats that pass by and more interested in utilising their own boat for travelling to destinations linked with business or retirement interests. The owner of this boat, named *Arm of the Union*, had fortunately berthed his boat here while going for a cycle and it was only in this location for an hour or two – though the photographer was certainly pleased with such a choice! The Pendolinos ply their own way to and fro at much greater speed than the canal craft that they pass and provide an impression of purpose and intent while enjoying their own version of Sunday afternoon exercise.

Above: Boston Lodge, Ffestiniog Railway, Monday 31 May 2004: 2-4-0STT *Linda* in light engine movement, with Traeth Mawr (Great Sand) Estuary in the background.

Representing a real pride of the Hunslet Engine Company, Leeds, which built *Linda* in 1893 for main-line service on the Penrhyn Quarry Railway, this locomotive exudes the very same awe and wonder in preservation, clearly seen here in immaculate condition in service with the Ffestiniog Railway. In 1970 *Linda* was converted to oil but in 2013 was converted back to coal. She is a very graceful locomotive, and is most appropriately located in the heart of Welsh mountain scenery as befits a locomotive which would have been found hard at work on the famed Penrhyn Quarry line in North Wales. It is still possible to walk along the old railway and see where *Linda* would have spent her days in industrial employment.

Opposite above: Exeter Stabling point, Friday 31 May 1985: Left, Class 31 31202, Class 33 33025 and a Class 47; right, Class 45 45069.

What a contrast between the mainly open-air servicing facility for the interesting variety of locomotives seen here, representing a typical if begrimed and functional snapshot from the 1980s, and the recent modernisation of this location with its brand new train maintenance depot. Here can now be found much-needed carriage wash and underframe cleaning facilities. The three internal roads within the depot support heavy maintenance (engine and bogie replacement) alongside general train access from mid- or high-level gantries for a variety of rolling stock. The impressive support block includes office spaces, meeting rooms, a staff canteen and welfare facilities for depot staff and train crew. With a serious spend of £40m it shows significant investment to provide the long awaited care and attention required by the local fleet of trains. Class 31s, one of which is seen here, worked to Barnstaple as part of their normal duties in the area. They were quite common on Exeter–Paignton stopping services and many reached Plymouth on various workings.

Below: Dinting, Thursday 2 June 1994: Class 305 EMU 305503 in newly applied Regional Railways livery departs with the 14.08 ex-Hadfield to Manchester Piccadilly.

Class 305 units were generally deployed on inner suburban services from London Liverpool Street to Chingford, Enfield Town and Hertford East. Some were later deployed in the Greater Manchester area, with a few specified for Hadfield services until track alignment was performed in 1997, allowing the longer bodied Class 323s to negotiate the sharp curves at Dinting station. They were therefore found operating along the western end of the famed Woodhead route as far as Hadfield. Pairs of Class 76 electrics on coal trains would have regularly passed over Dinting Vale Viaduct, seen ahead and looking to the west. It opened for traffic in 1844, and is 1,452ft (442m) long.

Stirling, Friday 2 June 2000: Class 156 in Strathclyde PTA carmine and cream livery departs with the 09.33 Edinburgh to Dunblane as it passes the 107-lever signal box north of the station.

Stirling had a most splendid set of former Caledonian Railway Company semaphore signals at the south end of the station and a fine bracket signal at the north end, as seen here. Modernisation in 2013 has seen all replaced by colour lights, however the station's heritage architecture remains intact and is worthy of closer inspection. The Stirling North signalbox which the train is passing is also a fine example of Caledonian Railway architecture, and dates from the 1900's. The carmine and cream livery set the Strathcyde regional train fleet apart and had its own appeal when kept clean. The blue skies suggest it's a fine day to the north, and there is that hint of special light that befits Scotland's appeal to photographers and landscape artists.

Opposite below: Hookhills Viaduct, Paignton and Dartmouth Railway, Wednesday 2 June 2004: Class 4MT 4-6-0 75014 *Braveheart* hauls the 14.00 Paignton to Kingswear.

Here's a preserved railway which enjoys the benefit of linking the key holiday resorts of Torbay with the historic port of Dartmouth, which is a real honeypot for visitors for most of the year round, partly thanks to the sailing fraternity. It is interesting that families on their Whit or summer holiday at Torbay will be prepared to forsake the golden sands in order to travel by steam train to a resort which is essentially a deep water harbour. There is the additional attraction at Dartmouth of the typical seaside shops and cafeterias of course, and a pleasant mile's walk will access Dartmouth Castle near the mouth of the River Dart.

Below: Saltern Cove, Torbay, Paignton and Dartmouth Railway, Wednesday 2 June 2004: Class 4MT 4-6-0 75014 *Braveheart* hauls the 16.15 Paignton to Kingswear.

The scenic beauty of Torbay rewards travellers along this railway, with its climb out of Goodrington revealing stunning views from the carriage window rather as when an artist slowly unveils their completed masterpiece. The fact that most trains are made up of seven carriages indicates the popularity of this railway with tourists and locals alike. One particularly busy week for the railway is during the Dartmouth Regatta at the end of August which attracts vast crowds from across the UK and internationally. There are over 300 sailing races and events during Regatta Week including 50 rowing heats and races. Its popularity is thanks to the varied celebrations which include air displays, sailing competitions, live music, street food, fireworks, water polo, barrel rolling, a waterborne treasure hunt and pavement artists. Parking is at such a premium in Dartmouth and nearby Kingswear that travel to and from the events by the steam railway is a preferred option and extra trains are provided into the evening at the Regatta weekend.

Above: Near Toddington, Gloucestershire Warwickshire Railway, Saturday 2 June 2007: Class 7F 2-8-0 53808 hauling the 17.12 Winchcombe to Toddington freight.

The bushy shrub on the left has produced its trademark blooms of creamy-white flowers. These are elderflowers which can add subtle flavours to accompanying grapes used in white wine for those who are into winemaking and homemade jam for those adventurous in their cuisine. They flower from May to June.

The crew of this locomotive may not be too concerned with such, although tales are told of remote branch line engine drivers in days of steam-hauled freight pausing at known locations to nip into adjacent fields to collect mushrooms and blackberries, or even to take home hares and rabbits for tea from friendly signal-box men! One can speculate whether such ever happened on the 'Slow and Dirty', as the Somerset and Dorset Joint Railway was sometimes known, and 53808, or S&D no. 88, was one of two surviving members of an original class of eleven designed for working heavy freight trains over the Mendip Hills. It mainly worked the local goods trains between Bath and Evercreech Junction – perhaps time for a spot of blackberry collecting in between duties wasn't out of the question?

Opposite: Bethany, Friday 4 June 2021: Great Western 'Castle' HST passes with the 13.46 Plymouth to Penzance.

This photograph is taken from the intriguingly named Padderbury overbridge. The evidence of the teams that have been lopping the lineside trees during the winter months is all too clear, and the railway cutting reveals a dash of blues, bright greens and pinks to reinforce that spring is well established at this late part of the season. The previous month of May had been persistently cool and wet throughout and the long-awaited very welcome blue skies and warm sunshine have certainly encouraged the blossoming flowers that are glimpsed by passengers travelling into Cornwall. As it is a Whit holiday weekday, many travellers will already be encamped on the multitude of beaches that the Cornish resorts boast, especially on the south coast. This is one of the shortened HST 'Castle' sets with three rather than the customary four carriages.

Above: TreBrown overbridge, Friday 4 June 2021: Great Western 'Castle' HST with the 13.18 Exeter St Davids to Penzance.

Seen just about to cross Tresulgan Viaduct with its six arches, this is very much Cornish main line territory with sharp curves and many viaducts, tree-lined embankments and cuttings, all contributing to the character of the Royal Duchy. Travellers are often puzzled by the fact that while they can travel the 225 miles from London Paddington to Plymouth in three hours, nearly a further two hours are required to reach Penzance at a distance of only 79.5 miles. However, a quick look at the rolling countryside and hills soon indicates the reason, for while there is much to appeal in terms of picturesque landscape, the contours encountered along the route dictate a more leisurely journey. While some see this as rather an endurance test, the upgraded comfort and quality of trains provided such as these 'Castle' HST sets surely mitigates any such inconvenience! TreBrown overbridge is also known as Menheniot Road Bridge.

Opposite: Coombe by Saltash Viaduct, Friday 5 June 2020: Colas Class 67 67023 and 67027 pass with the 12.01 Penzance to Paignton and Reading Triangle NMT.

This train is often worked by a specially adapted HST, also in Network Rail yellow livery, and records track condition information at speeds up to 125mph. It helps locate and identify faults before they become a safety issue or affect train performance and is equipped with the most up-to date high-tech measurement systems, track scanners and a high-resolution camera. As seen in a previous photograph, here it is again in the charge of two Colas Rail Freight Class 67 locomotives also used to power these infrastructure monitoring trains for Network Rail, though their appearance in the South West is less common. It makes a colourful splash of colour amidst the verdant greens of late spring which are slowly exerting themselves in the multitude of trees and bushes.

Opposite: Fawley Hill Railway, Sunday 6 June 2004: Hudswell Clarke 0-6-0 saddle tank no. 31 climbs the 1 in 14 gradient to Somersham station.

    This powerful little engine was built in 1913 and used in the construction industry, including the building of Wembley Stadium in the 1920s and at Llanwern Steel Works in the 1960s. It was the first locomotive to arrive at Fawley Hill in 1965. The standard gauge railway is a private garden railway and museum owned by the late Sir William McAlpine, now in the care of his widow, Lady Judy McAlpine. It is maintained by a dedicated team of volunteers and features many items of rolling stock. Somersham station was on the former St Ives to March line. There is also an impressive museum with plenty of railway memorabilia to keep visitors fascinated for hours.

Below: Nappers Halt, South Devon Railway, Saturday 9 June 2007: Class 04 D2246 is approaching with the 17.05 from Totnes to Buckfastleigh.

    The stock for this train is formed of two autocoaches with their exit doors located towards the west end of each carriage. A lever inside the coach door vestibule would be used to lower inbuilt steps for ease of access to low platforms and can be useful for dropping off track maintenance teams and equipment away from stations. They were especially useful on rural branch lines provided with local halts serving their sparse population. Lineside trees are in full leaf and the warm sun will be encouraging a myriad of insects to pollinate them for future generations.

Above: Staverton Weir, South Devon Railway, Saturday 9 June 2007: Class 31 31108 arrives with the 17.47 Totnes to Buckfastleigh.

Class 31 locomotives did haul trains in the south-west during BR days, though their origins were very much to be found in the Eastern Region. This locomotive was originally numbered D5526 and entered service for British Railways at Stratford depot, East London. It was based at several Eastern Region depots during its active life and on 9 June 2007 was preserved on the South Devon Railway by its owners, the A1A Locomotives Group. It looks very smart in early Railfreight light grey livery with 'wrap round' yellow cabs and a large BR logo in white on the side. The rampant spring growth has started to establish its presence in the 'four foot' and will need a visit by the line's weedkilling department.

Opposite above: Buckfastleigh, South Devon Railway, Saturday 10 June 2006: Class 37/3 37321 (ex-37037) departs with the 16.37 goods train for Totnes.

This Class 37 was based at several Eastern Region depots during the 1960s and 70s and was later allocated to Motherwell. These popular locomotives, characterised by their English Electric 'growl' when accelerating, have endured well beyond other locomotives of their generation and continue in main line use with Colas Rail, Direct Rail Services, Europhoenix, Network Rail and West Coast Rail, alongside a plethora of preserved railways. They are versatile yet powerful, and over the last decade have fulfilled such varied duties as rail head treatment trains or winter work in push/pull mode with snowploughs, in moving nuclear flasks or new rolling stock around the country such as the Elizabeth line Class 345s. They have seen recent service in charge of passenger trains along the Cumbrian Coast and in East Anglia working with hauled passenger coaches, much to the delight of the 'haulage' fraternity, replacing a shortfall in what would otherwise be timetabled services worked by DMUs. They represent a heritage design with their large front-end nose and some retain end gangways and split headcodes recalling these common features on locomotive classes from the 1960s.

Below: Near Washford, West Somerset Railway, Saturday 12 June 2010: Front, 'Western' Class 52 D1062 *Western Courier*, preserved at the Severn Valley Railway; second, 'Western' Class 52 D1010 *Western Campaigner*, preserved at the West Somerset Railway, hauling 12.00 Bishops Lydeard to Minehead.

What a fine sight, despite the efforts to intrude by a determined elderflower, proudly displaying twinned 'Westerns' in maroon livery with half-yellow warning panels and white cabs. Both locomotives were based at Oak Common, Landore, Laira and in the case of *Western Courier* Cardiff Canton. Their sleek, striking appearance is reinforced when paired in this way, although such events were most irregular in practice. It is a tribute to their restoration to working order in preservation that enthusiasts can enjoy the resilient sight and sound of these locomotives with their Maybach engines hard at work – an interesting reflection when at the time of their withdrawal from service, the priority of many preservationists remained focused on resurrecting steam locomotives and, as with the preserved 'Deltics', a loyal and committed fan base ensured their glamour was fully reinstated.

Above: Near Bicknoller, West Somerset Railway, Saturday 12 June 2010: 'Western' Class 52 D1010 *Western Campaigner*, preserved at the West Somerset Railway, hauling 17.00 Bishops Lydeard to Minehead.

Working in its more familiar style single-heading a late afternoon train below the fine vista of the Quantocks basking in the late afternoon sunshine, *Western Campaigner*'s livery fits in perfectly with the surrounding landscape. Diesel enthusiasts are regularly treated to mixed-traction galas where the line's preserved diesel fleet and visiting guest locomotives have the chance to stretch their legs over a 20-mile route past quintessential farms and thatched-roof houses, rolling hills and vistas over the Bristol Channel. The steady gradient from Williton on the return journey will allow 'Western' enthusiasts a chance to hear the locomotive's distinct hydraulic roar as it engages with the climb to Crowcombe and provides a similar opportunity to steam enthusiasts when hauled by one of the home fleet of steam locomotives based at the line, when they can hear the steady beat of the pistons and rods and the voluminous emission of steam and smoke belched out from the chimney.

Opposite: Staverton Weir, South Devon Railway, Sunday 13 June 2010: GWR 2251 class 0-6-0 3205 hauls the 15.22 Totnes to Buckfastleigh.

Viewed emerging from the sylvan glade, it was good to enjoy the sight and sound of this stablemate of the South Devon Railway's fleet of steam locomotives, providing an interesting contrast to the line's smaller pannier tanks. Painted in British Railways unlined green livery, it was returned to service in May 2010 although it has since been withdrawn from service after it was identified that it needed a major boiler rebuild and new cylinder block. The telegraph poles are a reminder of the days when these were located alongside railways to convey telegraph and telephone signals, although they were gradually replaced by conduited cables and had largely disappeared by the early 1980s.

Buckfastleigh, South Devon Railway, Saturday 13 June 2004: Class 127 Derby Suburban DMU 51592 and 51604, stabled.

Framed by the bracket signal at the down end of Buckfastleigh station platform, this diesel multiple unit represents the useful type of 'modern' lightweight train that was intended to provide the opportunity for rural or under-utilised branches to survive into the 1960s and beyond, after steam locomotives were deemed to be obsolete, with their greed for coal and at least two crew, and their requirement for turning at termini if not equipped for push and pull or if running as an auto-train. The Beeching era saw many such branches closed by stealth, with figures of the travelling public tweaked to look their worst after services were reduced to inconvenient times - much the same occurred on the Settle and Carlisle Railway in the 1980s. However, where these units did succeed, they provided a warm and comfortable environment for travellers requiring suburban and regional services. Preserved railways find them useful for supplying a service at off-peak times of the day and season, and a multitude of various types have been preserved, supplying a snapshot of the first generation diesel units on British Railways.

Opposite below: Buckfastleigh, South Devon Railway, Saturday 13 June 2004: Class 14 D9525 departs with an early afternoon freight.

Seen just crossing Mardle Bridge, the signal (applying to down trains arriving) behind the departing train to the rear is of much interest. The upper left signal is the Inner Home for the platform whereas the upper right is the Inner Home for the loop, which here is just out of sight. Below left is a 'calling on' Subsidiary signal for trains to enter the platform and below right is the 'shunt ahead' Subsidiary signal for the loop. Set to the right is the yard disc. The headcode displayed would normally have applied to an ordinary passenger or breakdown train, so this probably should be code 6E or 7F depending on whether there are four fitted vehicles in the train consist.

Below: Near Hood Bridge, South Devon Railway, Saturday 13 June 2004: Front, Class 20 20110 *River Dart*; second, Class 20 20118 *Saltburn by the Sea* pass with a mid-afternoon service from Totnes to Buckfastleigh.

The River Dart looks especially tranquil here but increasingly wet winters have seen the water level particularly high nearer to Dartington and close to overlapping the railway embankment. Furthermore, Nursery Pool Bridge, which takes the railway over the River Dart near Buckfastleigh, suffered damage to one of its piers during the wettest February on record. The reflections are only available when the flow of the water is slow; after very heavy rain or continuous wet weather, the very fast flow of the river rules out such photographic opportunities. Most canoeists avoid venturing out when the river is in full spate, although on a fine day such as this when the water is calm they can often be seen paddling along.

Near Hood Bridge, South Devon Railway, Saturday 13 June 2004: Class 14 D9525 passes with a mid-afternoon parcels train from Staverton to Buckfastleigh.

The contrast between this locomotive's previous locations of work in the Durham coalfield when D9525 worked for the National Coal Board, being based at several collieries, and that portrayed here could not be more vast. The type of duty carried out by this class was trip working movements between local yards and hauling short-distance freight trains. They were very useful for shunting duties with their all-around visibility provided by the cab and dual controls. They were reliable but their use in such traffic with British Railways became much reduced a few years after they came into use, hence this locomotive was sold to the NCB in 1968. It is one of nineteen examples preserved (two of which are presently on hire to industrial companies), which is a very high ratio for a class total of fifty-six, thus further demonstrating their sustained versatility.

Opposite below: Approaching Nappers Crossing, South Devon Railway, Saturday 13 June 2004: Class 127 Derby Suburban DMU, 51592 and 51604, passes with the 17.04 Buckfastleigh to Totnes.

The destination blind for the London terminus of St Pancras recalls the suburban route to Bedford that was served by these powerful DMUs. The speed whiskers adorning the front did add a colourful embellishment when applied, prior to the split yellow warning panels from the early-1960s. The requirement by British Railways for a full yellow end saw off such interesting embellishments. European railway practice abroad has for a long time seen locomotives wearing a multitude of liveries without such a yellow front requirement. More recently, headlight technology has improved so much that, if a lamp arrangement used on a locomotive or unit meets the minimum requirements in the Technical Specifications for Operability (TSI) – which require two headlamps, three marker lamps and two tail lamps, all of specific luminescent properties – then there is no longer any need for a yellow end, as demonstrated for example by the black ends of the new Elizabeth Line units.

Below: Hookhills Viaduct, Paignton and Dartmouth Steam Railway, Sunday 13 June 2021: GWR 5205 class 2-8-0T 5239 *Goliath* passes with the 12.25 Paignton to Kingswear.

It is a challenge to the use of the astronomical calendar when the picture representing spring as defined by the former suggests a summer's day, and indeed this day was blessed with full sunshine and late June warmth, though the steam trail reminds us that the middle of the day is not yet warm enough for the steam to disperse quickly in the heat. The concept of the genuine era of steam trains by the sea as being when the British summer holiday was essentially to the nearest or most accessible British coastline ignores the fact that many passengers travelled great distances from London and the Home Counties or the Midlands by fast express trains to either Dorset, Devon or Cornwall – and for many a youngster the thrill of the long journey hauled by a steam train in itself played a key role in the holiday experience as a whole. Memories of such golden summers days and trouble-free travel are no doubt selective, but we justifiably prefer to remember the best after all!

Above: Hookhills Viaduct, Paignton and Dartmouth Steam Railway, Sunday 13 June 2021: LMS 'Royal Scot' Class 7P 4-6-0 46100 *Royal Scot* crosses with the 09.07 Bristol Temple Meads to Kingswear 'English Riviera Express'.

A 'Royal Scot' locomotive pays tribute to shared royalty in the shape of the MS *Queen Victoria* just outside this picture, but seen in the background right of the previous photograph, with its gross tonnage of 90,000t. Each is a magnificent accolade to those who designed their characteristic features and maybe the crew of the locomotive will acknowledge such with a sharp whistle or two. Seen in an earlier image at Glyndyfrdwy, on the Llangollen Railway as featured on page 33, this location offers a somewhat different perspective overlooking Torbay at a time when cruise liners anchored in the shelter of the bay during the COVID-19 pandemic awaiting the lifting of travel restrictions uncomfortably close to the start of the summer season's anticipated sailings. Certainly the passengers on board the train can be thankful that they can fulfil their journey's delights – could it be that one or two are indeed hopefully booked to travel on the seas during the forthcoming season?

Opposite: Britannia Crossing, Kingswear, Paignton and Dartmouth Railway, Sunday 16 June 1991: Class 35 'Hymek' D7017 leads 'Western' Class 52 D1035 *Western Yeoman* as it approaches and passes with the 13.35 Kingswear to Paignton.

Here is a sight to enliven anyone with a passion for West Country diesel heritage. It's a pairing of two locomotives sharing Maybach engines and hydraulic transmission, both of which were synonymous with Western Region trains in the 1960s and 70s. Each class met slightly different requirements during their days of service on the Western Region. 'Hymeks' operated secondary passenger services based around Bristol, such as Paddington to Hereford and semi-fast services to the west of England and Wales. They were also eventually assigned to express trains, from London Paddington to Cardiff and Swansea services. As a mixed-traffic design, the 'Hymeks' also worked pickup freights throughout the Western Region alongside inter-regional passenger services. In comparison, the 'Westerns' were designed for fast express trains on mainline work to the West Country, with the capability of tackling the Devonian gradients with plenty of power to draw on. Their distinct designs set them apart from the early British Railways diesels operated by the other regions.

Chapter 2
SUMMER

Rattery, Saturday 20 June 1987: Class 47/4 47549 *Royal Mail* with the 09.58 Penzance to Leeds.
  Clearly summertime has arrived with a summer Saturday CrossCountry train with the locomotive in charge having emerged from Marley Tunnel (seen behind the train) to display its InterCity livery with the wrap-around yellow cab. This service would now be formed of either a CrossCountry Voyager or, if diagrammed, an HST set. Locomotive haulage provided greater variety of livery colours in the summer when freight or parcels sector locomotives might be drafted in where shortages occurred in order to meet the demands of the vastly increased summer Saturday timetable to and from the south-west.

Rattery, Saturday 20 June 1987: Class 50 50003 *Temeraire* in charge of the 08.38 London Paddington to Penzance.

It is a matter of interest that people allocate names of endearment to people they hold dear – and this seems to be the case for railway enthusiasts when adopting terms for railway locomotives too, especially diesels! Class 50s are referred to by the enthusiast community as 'Hoovers' because of the similarity of sound they emit to a hoover. Class 40 locomotives' English Electric engines do make a high pitch whistle indeed, hence their being referred to as 'Whistlers'. Class25 locomotives tended to run about on local freight and passengers turns, rather like a rat running around its business – hence their term 'Rats'. Those Class 33 locomotives allocated to the Hastings route to Ashford had to be built at reduced dimensions because several tunnels on the line had been bored to the minimum possible dimensions and lined so poorly that there was danger of collapse. Several extra layers of brick lining had to be added, as a result of which the tunnels were too narrow to accommodate standard-size stock. Thus the Hastings line had to be worked with specially-built stock of restricted dimensions. These Class 33s were hence called 'Slim Jims' while their unrestricted fellow locomotives were simply referred to as 'Cromptons' after their Crompton-Parkinson traction motors. During the 1970s and 1980s, Class 47s had an increasing tendency to break down and be unreliable, hence their being nicknamed 'Duffs'. Class 44 locomotives inherited their nickname 'Peaks' as they were formally named after mountains in the Peak and Lake District, North Yorkshire and Wales. This term has also tended to be extended to the similar Class 45s. Class 37s are 'Growlers' after their sound emitted when accelerating hard. Class 70s were initially disliked because of the unusual front cab design – hence their name, 'Ugly Duckling'. HSTs became 'Trams', no doubt after their sleek styling, and those painted in the InterCity blue and yellow were called 'Flying Bananas'. These are merely some of the highlights established by this trend.

Above: Churston Station, Paignton and Dartmouth Steam Railway, Saturday 20 June 1992: Class 50 50002/D402 with the 11.40 Kingswear to Paignton.

  It looks like this Class 50 has received a fresh coat of British Railways paint, and it enhances the sleek length of these fine locomotives. Their normal stamping ground wearing this livery prior to their move to West Country services was on the West Coast Main Line, and in the early 1970s they proved an awesome sight when paired ascending the gradients through the Lake District and onwards to Scotland up Beattock's challenging climb. In their final few years, these locomotives attracted as much admiration and dedication among the modern traction railway community as did the Class 52 'Westerns' in their heyday. Their opportunity to create some fine sound is amply catered for on the Paignton and Dartmouth line, with the 1 in 66 climb to Greenway tunnel from Kingswear and 1 in 60 to Churston from Goodrington. Passengers in the 'Devon Belle' observation carriage, built in 1917, may need earmuffs! The locomotive, preserved by the Devon Diesel Society, is currently under overhaul.

Opposite above: Britannia Crossing, Kingswear, Paignton and Dartmouth Steam Railway, Saturday 20 June 1992: Class 50 50002/D402 approaches with the 13.35 Paignton to Kingswear.

  Seen passing alongside the estuarial waters of the River Dart in this Sylvan setting, it is a reminder that the Class 50s would have regularly run alongside the waters of the Exe and Teign estuaries when in charge of mainline services to the West Country from the mid-1970s. Passengers enjoying the ride will here have a grandstand view over towards Dartmouth and the Britannia Royal Naval College on the far side of the Dart. The level crossing barriers are raised to permit traffic to cross on to the slipway that enables them to access the chain-guided Dartmouth Higher ferry.

Below: Britannia Crossing, Kingswear, Paignton and Dartmouth Steam Railway, Saturday 20 June 1992: Class 55 'Deltic' 55022/D9000 *Royal Scots Grey* approaches Kingswear with the 12.20 from Paignton.

Cars having crossed on to the slipway will need to be clear of the level crossing barriers, for the eastern ferry slipway of the Higher Ferry is immediately adjacent to the Britannia Crossing. Any rail enthusiasts among the car drivers not aware of the visiting locomotive's schedule will no doubt be taken aback by the sight of a 'Deltic' passing by! The two-tone green livery matches the verdant summer green leaves of the trees lining the hillside. The yachts moored in the river represent a very small fraction of those that are moored nearer to Dartmouth, where every size and shape of leisure boat can be viewed, from simple motor boats to luxury private cruisers, from impressive power boats to seagoing yachts.

Above: Hookhills Viaduct, Paignton and Dartmouth Steam Railway, Saturday 20 June 1992: Class 50 50002/D402 with late afternoon engineers' train from Paignton to Kingswear.

The sweep of Torbay provides a fine backdrop to this preservation-era demonstration train, with its small load hardly tasking the six English Electric traction motors with which it is equipped. It's certainly an early summer's day, no doubt attracting the more local residents to the beaches and coves, for national school holiday dates mean the crowds don't descend on the south-west until mid-July. This Class 50 would have had its share of hauling the summer Saturday holiday main line trains to and from the West Country, although without the hefty gradients encountered during its north-west sojourns, there would have been no need to be paired with another Class 50 to fulfil its BR Western Region duties.

Opposite above: Kingswear, Paignton and Dartmouth Steam Railway, Saturday 20 June 1992: Class 55 'Deltic' 55022/D9000 *Royal Scots Grey* in light engine movement after being detached from ECS.

'Deltics' have attracted as much of a steadfast following during the preservation era as that evident when in service during BR days. On Saturdays and in the holidays, the ends of York station platforms would be thronged with devotees arrayed with cameras and notebooks to record the scheduled and additional services on which 'Deltics' appeared. Others would be travelling behind the locomotives collating the speeds achieved and measuring their performance in everyday practice on the East Coast Main Line. In their latter days, when some were allocated to working the TransPennine route, on through trains from Liverpool Lime Street to York and Newcastle, the clamour for pursuing such appearances grew ever more intense. After all, what could beat the noise of a westbound 'Deltic' starting out of Huddersfield station and immediately being absorbed by the sounds of the Napier engines building to a crescendo which resounded off the Huddersfield tunnel walls? Maybe the same when entering Gasworks and Copenhagen tunnels just after leaving London Kings Cross? Passengers aboard the return service to Paignton behind *Royal Scots Grey* will be able to capture that same spirit on the climb up to Greenway Tunnel.

Below: Approaching Polbathic Bridge, near St Germans: DBS Class 66 66185 leads with 66192 at rear, with a Westbury to Lostwithiel civil engineers' train associated with replacing trackwork on the Fowey branch.

The western edge of Dartmoor can be seen in the background. The rolling countryside of east Cornwall enjoys the warmth of the summer sun and the Class 66 looks clean with maybe a recent lick of paint. There's quite a gradient here which taxes down trains such as this, but there's no rush as it has been fitted in behind a stopping service, although with a train every half hour into Cornwall, there is every reason to keep to the schedule dictated.

Wylye, Tuesday 22 June 2021: Great Western Class 158 three-car DMU passes the poppy fields with the 10.41 Great Malvern to Brighton service.

  The picturesque River Wylye flows through a gentle Wiltshire valley past some tranquil and colourful villages and countryside which is shared with the branch line from Westbury to Salisbury. At this time of the summer, the poppies are in full bloom and add a carpet of colour to the tapestry of this pleasant rural retreat. The season for poppies could be said to be autumn, when Remembrance Day recalls the lives lost and blood shed by countless soldiers in the wars that claimed so many lives in the twentieth century as well as other wartime combat losses since. Here they offer a retreat in the solitude of the surrounding countryside.

Restormel Manor Bridge, Saturday 26 June 2010: CrossCountry 'Super Voyager' Class 221 passes with the 07.00 Manchester Piccadilly to Newquay.

Cumulonimbus clouds are gathering over Bodmin in response to the build up of heat on this very warm day. Holidaymakers at Newquay, this train's destination, probably need not worry as the coastal breeze there will keep the clouds from becoming intrusive and spoiling the sunbathing. These trains are relatively photogenic but their cramped interiors and shabby condition – the result of intense use and heavy loadings on the populous parts of the network that they serve – paint a different picture. There will be very little room on board for the variously sized surfboards heading for Newquay's particular surfing attraction at Fistral Beach, with its west-facing direction which exposes it to large Atlantic swells that provide consistent waves throughout the year.

Forder Viaduct, Saturday 29 June 2002: Class 58 58021 *Hither Green Depot* in BR Mainline Freight blue livery hauls Pathfinder Tours' 'Cornish Explorer' from Birmingham International to Penzance.

Summer sees a variety of excursions to the West Country, some of which reach the furthest west destination at Penzance, and these are often powered by some unusual visiting locomotives. Class 58 locomotives were generally found at work with heavy block trains of hopper wagons in the east and north Midlands, operating merry-go-round circuits between collieries and power stations, although in later life they also operated tanker and stone trains. It is likely that this train is travelling to the far west of Cornwall for the passengers to enjoy the Mazey Day celebrations. Traffic is banished from Penzance's main shopping streets for the day, stalls line the pavements, there's a variety of street acts, and the main thoroughfare is bedecked with greenery gathered that same morning. Colourful processions move through the town, the most impressive of which includes themed costumes and an array of spectacular giant effigies created by local primary-school children in the area. These are paraded with excitement and pride, and enchant the large crowds. An additional attraction is the range of musical performances, many with a Celtic feel, and there is always a contingent of fellow Celts from France's Breton community.

Wearde Quay, Saturday 29 June 2002: Class 47/7 47726 *Manchester Airport Progress* in Rail Express Systems (RES) livery in charge of an excursion from Swansea to Par (for the Eden Project), utilising the green 'Ocean Liner' coaching set.

The parcels sector locomotives were occasionally used for relief passenger duties and here is one such example, although unusually working a variant liveried set of carriages. These Mk 1s are from the original Rail Charter Services (EWS) 'Southern Green' set. Par is a favoured destination for excursions because of the nearby Eden Project which can easily be visited within the time frame allowed before the diagrammed return time. There are two 'biomes', one of which is the Rainforest Biome in which you can *really* feel the tropical heat and experience four of the world's rainforest environments: Tropical Islands, Southeast Asia, West Africa and Tropical South America. You can walk along the canopy walkway, which takes you high over the treetops, along a rope bridge and through the swirling vapours of the 'Cloud Bridge'. You will see banana and cacao trees and, if very lucky, plants that flower for just one day a year in spectacular fashion. The author used to take high ability year 9 students, not always the most compliant of customers, and they would be mesmerised by the venue, their consequent creative and problem solving skills applied to a task set by the Eden Project education department fully vindicating the visit.

Bishops Bridge signal box, South Devon Railway, Monday 2 July 2001: Port Talbot Railway 0-6-0ST 813 in light engine movement around stock of Plymouth Railway Circle Special. No. 813 was visiting on loan from the Severn Valley Railway.

The light summer evenings permit such visits as seen here, one of several outdoor fixtures provided by the Plymouth Railway Circle, offering members a chance to travel along the preserved line, after the day's timetabled service has finished, in either brake vans or coaching stock and to catch on camera the gentle evening sunlight as it bathes the locomotive in such a way as to highlight the Great Western green livery. Here it occupies the up main line and may be waiting for the up main starting signal to give the road back to the coaching stock in Staverton station platform. It was one of nine 0-6-0 saddle tanks supplied between 1898 and 1901 to the Port Talbot Railway & Docks Company for shunting and trip working. The GWR entered into an agreement with the Port Talbot Railway in 1908 under which it took over operation of the Port Talbot Railways (excluding the docks' Port Talbot locomotives) when this locomotive as number 26 was added to GWR stock. It didn't receive its GWR number 813 until emerging from Swindon works in March 1924. After withdrawal it saw later service with collieries in the north-east of England. In its preservation era, it has been substantially restored at the Severn Valley Railway.

Waterside, Paignton and Dartmouth Steam Railway, Tuesday 20 July 2021: USATC Class S160 2-8-0 2253 passes with the 16.40 Kingswear to Paignton.

In 26°C this locomotive still manages to emit a wisp of steam on its descent past Torbay's fine vista. The problem for the railway company of course is that the majority of tourists will either be at the beaches, water sports venues or chilling in the shade of their cabins with a cooling drink at hand – not travelling inside very warm railway carriages! Any chance to refresh by splashing in the sea in such temperatures will prove very tempting, and reminds us that when rare heatwaves occur in the UK, there is no need to travel to continental destinations – not that such was at all possible on this occasion during the COVID-19 restrictions which were more than enough to discourage the majority of intrepid travellers and Mediterranean sunseekers. Quickly forgotten is the preceding unseasonably cool weather which had dampened everything. The locomotive could be heard from afar with its distinctive American chime whistle advertising its presence to those taking advantage of the nearby rock pools, and especially when soon passing Goodrington Sands.

Cockwood Harbour, Sunday 25 July 2010: First Great Western Class 143 crosses the causeway operating the 17.04 Paignton to Exeter St Davids.

The causeway is seen at its best at high tide, although the tidal inflow has floated the seaweed which limits the opportunity for a full reflection. These 'Pacer' diesel railcars were a slight improvement to the earlier Class 142 versions, and their bodies were built by Alexander, a bus company which had a good reputation for quality bus bodywork design. Given a refurbish in later years, they were almost tolerable to ride, and indeed were kept in service along the Barnstaple, Exmouth and Torbay branch lines much longer that intended owing to a continuing shortage of more modern stock cascaded from other parts of the country (such as 'Thames Turbos' from the North Downs line). However, with their relatively high entrance step, from 1 January 2020 they could only operate when paired with a PRM (person of reduced mobility) compliant Class 150 for such services as seen here when linking Exeter to Exmouth and Paignton. This was in order to meet the legal requirement for all rail operators to ensure all trains in service are fully accessible for disabled passengers. Final withdrawal from the area came in mid-December 2020.

Rye, Friday 27 July 2001: Preserved Class 201/202 Hastings DEMU Unit 1001 in BR green operating the 11.31 Hastings to Ashford.

This unit was preserved at St Leonards Railway Engineering and on hire to Connex South Central owing to a shortage of the usual fleet of Class 205/207s. It was one of a class built to slim proportions to accommodate the 'Hastings gauge'. The contractors for the 32-mile Tonbridge to Hastings line, Fox, Henderson & Co., had been having financial difficulties (the firm went bankrupt in 1857) and had tried to reduce losses by installing only four courses of bricks in the tunnels along the line. Given the enormous expense involved in rebuilding one of the most extensive tunnel systems in England, the South Eastern Railway solved the problem by installing two additional courses of bricks. This inevitably reduced the loading gauge of the line, and it was thereafter necessary to build narrow rolling stock such as the aforementioned 'Slim Jim' Class 33s. For their part the DEMUs were nicknamed 'Thumpers' because of the sound emitted by their English Electric traction motors which literally sounded as if they were thumping at something.

The Romney Marsh landscape through which the train will pass is one of sheep farms in squelchy flat fields, sluice gates and rather desolate atmospheric villages, peppered with distinct churches, and these elements almost envelop the BR Southern green unit as it plies its onward way east of Rye.

Lelant, Wednesday 28 July 2010: First Great Western Class 150/2 150233 paired with a second First Great Western Class 150/2 arrives with the 11.55 St Ives to St Erth as it runs alongside Hayle Estuary.

This station served as a park & ride station before a new car park was provided at St Erth. It was a popular boarding point as St Ives has very limited parking and road access. Tickets purchased from Lelant included the park & ride price, although there was no ticket machine supplied at the platform. The guard would be particularly busy on sunny summer holiday weekdays and weekends selling these tickets to the many passengers boarding there, with a relatively short journey time in which to complete this task. The unusual ticketing arrangements in the days of Wessex Trains however did not cater for those who chose to walk the coastal route one way to St Ives and return by train to Lelant, therefore making a single journey. The ticket machine had no such code entered for this type of journey and the author, undertaking such a trip, recalls a lively discussion with the guard who simply stated she could not sell a single ticket for the journey. The reader is left to conclude who won the debate …

New Romney, Romney, Hythe and Dymchurch Railway, Monday 29 July 2002: 4-6-2 no.1 *Green Goddess* in LNER green, built 1925, arrives with the 17.30 from Hythe.

The level of authenticity in this 15in (381mm) gauge *Green Goddess*, portraying its full-size sister locomotives, is very admirable. There is resplendent detail in the LNER apple green colour scheme and the intricate design details of the famous 4-6-2 'Pacific' A1 class locomotives which it magnificently imitates. There are in fact seven other 'Pacific' locomotives providing service on this line – a tribute to the appeal and flexibility of the 4-6-2 design in steam days. Also remarkable is the *Green Goddess* build date of 1925. Large-scale miniature railways have a special appeal to the general public, in the same way as miniature villages or parks. The level of miniaturised detail in the lineside signals and buildings is only compromised by the real-sized seating bench that no doubt has proved a welcome perch for awaiting passengers. The trains reach speeds on this route which imitate that which would be achieved by true expresses on the mainline – a most exhilarating ride!

Teignmouth, Thursday 30 July 2020: Class 70 70812 passes with the 07.17 Moorswater to Aberthaw cement train.

The beach is relatively quiet on this fine summer's day, with only a few joggers out for their daily exercise along the wall. Bearing in mind that it is the first full week of the school summer holidays, that is surprising. Meanwhile, on the same day, beaches on the south coast accessible to day trippers from London and the Home Counties were apparently packed! It may all have been owing to the presence of COVID-19, for no vaccines had yet been approved for use at this stage in the pandemic, and there was a very cautious approach to travel at least in the south-west. The presence of frequent trains along the sea wall at Dawlish and Teignmouth featured prominently in the author's childhood summer holidays in South Devon – for while the family remained on the beach, a certain youngster was carefully monitoring each and every train that passed, and with 'Westerns', 'Peaks' and 'Hymeks' at the helm, they all made a big impression on this viewer!

St Erth, Friday 7 August 1998: A pair of Class 150 units in Regional Provincial livery transfer from the St Ives branch to run down the up main line with the 19.30 St Ives to Penzance. Six trains each weekday at this time were diagrammed for this move, with four on Saturdays.

It is always nice to see semaphore signals and traditional signal boxes on parade, and there are still a few dotted around Cornwall – perhaps because the priority to replace them is somewhat lower than nearer the Home Counties?! In later BR days, much of the signalling in Cornwall was rationalised, with many boxes being closed and long block sections created. A desire to increase services in Cornwall for summer 2019 was eventually enabled by retaining the existing signal boxes, shortening the block sections to create around a six-minute headway, modernising some of the level crossings and using the recently provided telecom transmission links to join it all up. No doubt Cornish branch lines would all be operated by radio signalling if the trend was like that found in some European countries, but there are certain bastions of semaphore signals in Germany, at least.

The cloudless skies promise fine weather for the next day's crowds, and being a summer Saturday, the strengthened service to St Ives, with longer trains provided, will be very busy. It will also be a changeover day for the resort's hotels, with contented guests returning up country during the morning and new guests arriving hopefully in the afternoon. There is good reason to be hopeful too: summer timetables nowadays seem to run smoothly and there isn't the traffic jam of trains arriving from points east and north as there was during the 1960s and 70s, when motorail (car-carrying trains operating long distance routes), parcels, excursions and relief trains all had to fit in with the strengthened Saturday timetable. All good fun to watch and definitely fodder for camera-toting rail enthusiasts.

Above: St Erth, Friday 7 August 1998: Virgin HST set arrived with the late running 06.39 Dundee to Penzance 'The Cornishman'. The St Ives branch Class 150 is seen on the left.

In view of the distance covered, and potential bottlenecks in Edinburgh, Yorkshire and the Midlands, late running of this train can probably be allowed for. The St Ives branch trains however do run very punctually. This has been seen to be of detriment to connections from down services, where the train arrives just a few minutes late and over a hundred passengers alight to cross the footbridge and join the branch line train only to see it depart literally as they walk over the bridge. An 'interesting' discussion followed with the booking clerk at St Erth who suggested that the important businessman or woman at St Ives could not afford to have their train to St Erth run late from St Ives as they might miss their London train (which of course will be running to time despite a ten-minute connection being allowed). The despondent passengers for St Ives must, however, wait over half an hour for the branch train to reappear for their next available service. Surely timetable planning can do better than this?

Opposite above: Teign Estuary, Teignmouth, Tuesday 11 August 1998: An RES livery Class 47/7 with matching livery on vans on a mid-afternoon north-bound parcels train which may be bound for the north-east.

There is a fence along here now, though at least not of the steel palisade variety. Passengers travelling between Teignmouth and Newton Abbot can enjoy an unimpeded view over the wide estuary, and near here, just north of the narrow river mouth, can be seen people collecting cockles, clams and oysters at low tide. Maybe even some of that seaweed ends up on local restaurant plates! The small port, where the cranes can be seen in the background, handles ball clay and animal feed, grain, stone chippings, salt and forestry products. It accommodates vessels up to 90m in length and up to 6m in draft on the highest spring tides. There are four working berths, which are fully equipped to handle the wide range of cargoes for both import and export.

Below: Starcross, Tuesday 11 August 1998: InterCity Class 47/4 with the 08.40 Glasgow Central to Penzance. This long distance service is on time and the Class 47 looks proudly in charge with its smart and clean coat of paint. The red livery of the Virgin CrossCountry carriages assists a streamlined image and each livery complements the other. The tide is out leaving the sands and rivulets leading to the Exe for the various dippers, waders and gulls to enjoy a spot of tea – in this case, fish, although the seagulls may well have an eye on those eating chips with their fish on the nearby prom . It is certainly known for them to use any opportunity to grab a full bag of chips or a nice iced bun, or ice-cream cornet before the frustrated victim has a chance to respond. When eating by the seaside, beware!

Starcross, Tuesday 11 August 1998: Front, Class 37/0 37262 *Dounreay* in plain grey livery; second, Class 37/0 37156 in Transrail livery with a northbound china clay train, late afternoon.

This train is seen passing the Grade I listed 'Brunel's Atmospheric Railway' engine and pumping house, built in 1845. It was built as part of the South Devon Atmospheric Railway, which was projected to run between Exeter and Plymouth. Constructed of ashlar red sandstone, it was built in Italianate style as were of all the pumping houses on the line. The tower and chimney were reduced in height by 50ft (15m) after storm damage in the late nineteenth century. The innovative design concept involved a system which did not use locomotives, instead the trains were moved by 'atmospheric' (vacuum) traction, with the air being extracted from pipes laid between the rails by stationary engines at a series of pumping stations along the line. However, it was flawed from the outset because of the reliance on the use of leather flaps to seal the air pipes. The leather had to be kept supple by the use of tallow, and tallow is attractive to rats. These gnawed through the leather hence the vacuum could not be maintained, and the air-powered vacuum service lasted less than a year, from 1847 to 10 September 1848.

Cockwood Harbour, Tuesday 11 August 1998: HST power cars in contrasting liveries of Great Western Trains "Merlin" Swallow livery and InterCity, with an intermediate barrier vehicle pass on an eastbound test run from Laira depot, early evening.

Here's an interesting train formation and the drivers along here must enjoy the scenery despite knowing their route well. The question of which liveries best suited the HST power cars over the years has proved interesting. The most recently applied Great Western livery looks traditional and smart but doesn't help if photographed against a green or dark background. Some favoured the First Great Western blue livery, the dynamic lines of which were eye-catching and jazzy, others the blue and yellow which adorned HSTs when first introduced to service. There is no questioning that the Virgin Trains East Coast livery, which looks equally attractive on Class 91 locomotives and it's successor LNER livery applied to 'Azumas', also won the approval of the enthusiast community once applied to that fleet of HSTs. It may be that the InterCity livery shown in this picture was better suited to locomotives than HST power cars. The choice of livery will always be subjective, but the applied livery is an essential ingredient of the manner in which a railway company presents itself. The much disdained ONE livery which adorned trains belonging to the Greater Anglia franchise which sought to combine all of the services operating out of London Liverpool Street (reflecting the union of the three previous smaller franchises into one single franchise) just proves that livery makes an important statement and unavoidably invites a response.

Cockwood Harbour, Tuesday 11 August 1998: RES livery Class 47/7 with matching livery on vans, early evening on the 1E41 17.23 Plymouth to Low Fell parcels train, including a four-car PCV set at rear.

Here's a reminder of the colourful parcels sector trains which plied their way over long distances in the UK, saving many lorries making such journeys, often overnight, and facilitating the logistics of a reliable service which the trains ensured. In the early 1990s, the British Rail parcels sector Rail Express Systems required some driving trailers which could work in push-pull mode with their Class 47s. This would avoid the need to change the locomotive to other end of the train when it had arrived at its terminus, all of which took precious time. These new vehicles were called' Propelling Control Vehicles' (PCVs), as they would only be used to propel a train into or out of a terminus, and not used at high speed or over long distances. At the time, many redundant Class 307 overhead EMU vehicles were stored at various locations around the country after withdrawal from Eastern Region suburban services operating from London Liverpool Street, and these were selected for conversion. Hunslet-Barclay in Kilmarnock gained the contract for the rebuilding work which included removal of the windows and slam-doors, the fitting of roller-shutter doors and modernisation of the cab. Royal Mail 'Postal' Class 325 EMUs still provide a service between Royal Mail's Princess Royal Distribution Centre (PRDC) in Willesden, North London, to and from Warrington and Shieldmuir mail terminals. These carry a livery of Post Office red, with two yellow stripes running along the lower bodyside before turning sharply backwards and pointing up towards the roof, black cab window surrounds and a full yellow warning panel.

Lancaster, Thursday 13 August 2009: DRS Class 66/4 66434 passes at 09.27 with a Stobart Rail container train, 06.12 Daventry to Grangemouth.

The privatised sector certainly adds colour to the UK rail scene, both in the passenger and freight divisions. The DRS livery is eye-catching, and well suits the horizontal lines of the Class 66 locomotives. The company evidently takes much pride in keeping its fleet clean – and not just the paintwork! The Stobart containers in this train consist advertise the fact that their conveyance uses 'less CO2', referring to the amount of that greenhouse gas emitted if the same merchandise was delivered by a large fleet of lorries battling their way up the ever-congested M6. Passenger railway companies are also keen to promote their 'greener' environmental impact. The author is informed by Great Western that a journey by train from Plymouth to Teignmouth will give a 68% CO2 emission saving of 2.2kg CO2 based on one person travelling this journey by train and not by car.

Holywell, Thursday 19 August 1993: Class 37/4 37414 *Cathays C&W Works 1846–1993* in Regional Railways livery hauls the 13.30 'The Irish Mancunian' Holyhead to Manchester Victoria, here a substitute for a Class 158 during the summer peak.

The train has just passed Holywell Junction signal box, and the disused station, which was closed on 14 February 1966. The summertime locomotive-hauled trains along the North Wales Coast during the early to mid-1990s may have been favoured by rail enthusiasts for their haulage by either Class 37 or 31 locomotives, but they fulfilled an important role in providing adequate capacity for the hordes of holidaymakers, notably from the Midlands and cities in the north-west, who descended on the region during the peak of the summer holidays when the factories and schools had closed down. The fact that the North Wales main line railway served several holiday resorts which had long sandy beaches (and jellyfish!) helped reduce road usage and to transport quickly and comfortably those families who did not own a car.

Holywell, Thursday 19 August 1993: Class 37/4 37422 *Robert F. Fairlie Locomotive Engineer 1831–1885* in Regional Railways livery hauls the 14.30 Holyhead to Crewe.

On the same day as the previous photograph, and only an hour later, another service, in the same direction, passes through Holywell. Of course the intense summer diagrams required the traction supplied to meet the timetabled services at whatever time the schedule demanded. It's all quite a history lesson with at least four semaphore signals evident alongside the railway architecture at this location, a dedicated livery to locomotives and stock, and the pride bestowed on the locomotives of wearing a nameplate. Modernisation tends to sweep all away and with it so much of the railway atmosphere. The expectation to move such vast crowds has, of course, been much reduced by the rapid increase in cheap air fares and package holidays to a multitude of destinations in the guaranteed warm and sunny climes of the southern Mediterranean. Day visits to the North Wales coast tend now to be the norm, and nearby Chester itself is a very popular tourist attraction and shopping centre.

Strathpeffer, Saturday 23 August 2003: Highland Railway station terminus.

The Highland Railway station was a terminus at the end of a short branch from the line between Dingwall and Kyle of Lochalsh. It opened on 3 June 1885 and closed on 23 February 1946 to passengers (26 March 1951 to freight). Initially it was served by seven trains a day each way from nearby Dingwall, though during the Second World War this had dwindled to just four, and became very infrequent thereafter, with the inevitable closure to passengers following soon after.

Strathpeffer Spa was very popular during Edwardian times. A through sleeping car was operated from London Euston when the Spa was at its height of popularity. The single platform terminus building was provided with a booking office, waiting rooms, lavatories, a parcels office and a railway telegraph office. It is now occupied by craft shops and cafeterias. The varnished timber weatherboarding, twelve cast-iron decorated pillars and broad canopy spanning the platform, which is generously glazed by large multi-paned windows, all recall a style of station architecture which was as aesthetically appealing as it was functional. There would probably be a single line platform with an inadequate bus shelter supplied had the branch survived to the present, although it is ironic that this largest centre of population west of Dingwall is not served by the Kyle line!

Opposite below: Kyle of Lochalsh, Erbusaig Bay, Monday 25 August 2003: ScotRail Class 158 departs with the 11.52 to Inverness and Edinburgh.

This route from Kyle along the coastline – where the rocky outcrops meet the emerald blues and greens of the sea and the lofty mountains of Skye congregate in the distance like some prehistoric dinosaur – offers passengers a special encounter with the breathtaking beauty of this Scottish seascape splendour. The drivers of the trains of course will also pass by in the wettest and coldest weather of midwinter when it will look far less inviting. However, on a day like this, like a precious jewel, it is simply there to be enjoyed and admired. No wonder the scenic railways of Scotland draw tourists from the furthest realms of the globe.

Below: Carbis Bay, Thursday 26 August 1993: A pair of Pressed Steel Class 117 DMU units (the rear a three-car set, the front a two-car set) passes by the expanse of St Ives Bay operating the 15.47 St Ives to Lelant Saltings.

This train was timetabled to shuttle between Lelant Saltings, for the park & ride facility, and St Ives. It represents the first generation of DMUs, this design being provided with slam doors to each seating bay. They offered a firm and comfortable ride, although acceleration was definitely cautious. When introduced they would have replaced steam- or diesel-hauled coaching stock and would have appealed to drivers with their clean and improved driving environment, simplified controls and efficient heating. They were cost efficient in that there was no need for a locomotive to run around the stock at each end of the journey, and their gangway between carriages facilitated the work of the guard. Many preserved railways retain either single railcars or units with two or three carriages such as this one. They usually fulfil duties at quieter times of the day and season. When adorned with the BR green livery and speed whiskers on the front, they conveyed a sense of identity and purpose. Such was not to be the case with the 'Pacers' which replaced many of them during the 1980s.

Above: Berwick-upon-Tweed, Tuesday 26 August 2003: GNER Class 91 crosses the Royal Border Bridge with the 15.00 London King's Cross to Edinburgh and Glasgow Central, 'The Scottish Pullman'.

Built between 1847 and 1849 by Robert Stephenson, this grandiose sweeping twenty-eight-arch viaduct, of which thirteen arches span the river with fifteen overland to the south of the river at Tweedmouth, expresses an unabashed statement and purpose that nothing will stand in the way of the main line railway as it strides northwards to link England to Scotland (even if the border is a little further north of Berwick station). The reflection of the 38m height of the arches is well captured from the north bank of the River Tweed when the viaduct is bathed in early evening light which imbibes it with a golden hue. The sleek train, fully adorned in the GNER livery of dark, bold blue, with a flash of red and gold lettering, pays its own tribute to the engineering marvel over which it smoothly glides.

Opposite above: Forth Bridge, Saturday 5 September 2020: Viewed from Queensferry.

A hint that summer's heat is receding is indicated by the coats and jackets being worn during lunchtime, despite the strong sunlight. The clear air provides a further indication of such – for with heat there would be a haze. The Victorian masterpiece is seen in its full magnificence striding across the Firth of Forth with grace and determination, its highest point standing 110m above high water and 137m above its foundation. Functionally it enabled the East Coast railway route from London to extend north towards Aberdeen, and provided a much needed fixed link from Edinburgh to the Fife coast. As an icon of spectacular wonder, it has inspired and impressed generations of artists, writers and engineers from within their diverse fields. A photograph can but hint at the remarkable history and human triumph achieved in its awesome design and realisation, for it expresses the spirit of human endeavour and enterprise, of meeting any challenge with imagination, persistence and fortitude. Such qualities are here exemplified by pure brilliance.

Below: Banavie, Wednesday 9 September 2020: LMS Class 5MT 4-6-0 45407 passes over the Caledonian Canal with the 10.15 Fort William to Mallaig 'Jacobite'.

Looking as if it means business in tackling the demands of the West Highland gradients and wild mountain valleys that lie ahead, this Stanier 'Black 5' crosses the Caledonian Canal, Scotland's longest inland waterway with its 60 miles of navigable passage. The canal provided a long hoped-for route for mariners through the lochs Dochfour, Ness, Oichy and Lochy, between eastern and western Scotland, avoiding the long and often hazardous route round the west of Scotland and through the Pentland Firth. It is one of the many highlights of the journey taken by the 'Jacobite', which operates from late April through to late October with an additional afternoon service until the end of September. As such it traverses three seasons, and the autumn running dates allow late-season travellers to enjoy the unrivalled autumnal golds that adorn the trees and valleys of this spectacular scenic railway. Even at this date in September, hints of those colours are evident in the mountain grasses in the background.

Above: Corfe Common, Swanage Railway, Sunday 12 September 2010: SR 4-6-2 West Country 'Pacific' 34070 *Manston*, with the 13.50 Swanage to Norden.

It's a fine late summer's day and there is just a hint of the russet browns of the forthcoming autumn in the grass and heather. The red berries of late summer correspond well with the British Railways Brunswick green with red lining on the locomotive as it passes by the undulating Purbeck Hills in the background. The Railway Executive apparently described the livery as 'Dark Green lined Black and Orange'. The occupants of the Southern green carriages may be oblivious to it but to modellers it is an interesting aspect of livery detail, as the manufacturers of model railway engines know only too well!

Opposite: Corfe Common, Swanage Railway, Sunday 12 September 2010: A close up of rear locomotive LBSCR 0-6-0T Class A1 'Terrier' 32662 *Martello*, and a view of leading locomotive LSWR Class M7 0-4-4T 30053, working in push/pull mode on the 14.24 Harman's Cross to Norden.

No. 32662 *Martello* had earlier run out of water at Harman's Cross and so remained attached for watering at Corfe. The locomotive was one of a type rebuilt to A1X in 1912 with new boilers and extended smokeboxes. These diminutive tank locomotives were designed in 1870 to haul commuter trains on the heavily congested lines in South and South-East London. They lasted longer than most classes of pre-grouping tank engine under the Southern Railway, mainly because they were very well suited to working on several light railways which came under the Southern's administration at the grouping, such as the lines from Tenterden as well as on the Isle of Wight. No. 32662 in its earlier days saw service in London for suburban duties but by 1925 was proving useful on the Hayling Island branch. It is preserved at Bressingham Steam Museum.

Corfe Common, Swanage Railway, Sunday 12 September 2010: Leading locomotive LBSCR 0-6-0T Class A1 'Terrier', 32662 *Martello*; rear locomotive, GWR 0-6-2T 5600 class 6695 push/pull locomotives with the 14.50 Norden to Harman's Cross.

Both engines here engage with the gradient with resulting exuberant smoke and steam, making a marvellous sound to match. For their load of two carriages this may seem excessive but none of the assembled photographers are making any complaints. The resplendent Marsh umber livery carried by *Martello* proudly represents the livery which adorned these locomotives in the William Stroudley & Robert Billinton periods. The Purbeck Hills appear somewhat imposing to the small engine and emphasise the diminutive proportions of scale. Advocates of the theory that 'small is beautiful' certainly have a valid point with such engines as the 'Terriers' which have attracted reverent respect with their character and personality during steam days and in preservation – a feature with which the larger engines tend to compete less favourably.

Corfe Common, Swanage Railway, Sunday 12 September 2010: GWR 4-6-0 7800 'Manor' class 7802 *Bradley Manor* hauls the 15.10 Norden to Swanage.

Great Western locomotives have always commanded their own respect from the travelling public and devoted enthusiasts alike, and this custom has continued in the preservation scene. Where a railway promotes a Grouping-themed fleet of locomotives which is *not* Great Western, then the appearance of a Great Western locomotive certainly provokes significant interest, and this train looks like it has a full complement of passengers who are not just setting out for a day at Swanage's beaches and cafes, for it is mid-afternoon. They are enjoying the privilege of riding behind a visiting Great Western locomotive, while the usual steeds of LSWR locomotives are deployed on other services. It would be an interesting exercise to measure whether this Great Western magnetism is also reflected on preserved railways in the North of the UK as much as in the South.

Thursday 16 September 2021: LMS Class 5MT 4-6-0 45212 passes over the River Lochy Viaduct shortly after leaving Fort William with the 10.15 to Mallaig 'Jacobite'.

This ever-popular train is always fully booked for the two services that operate daily through the summer, as also seen in the previous picture on page 117. The magnet that draws the most photographers is, of course, the Glenfinnan Viaduct, which features in the spring section of photographs, to which coachloads of tourists – many clad in sandals or basic shoes and carrying their mobile phone cameras – trek along the hillside footpath to view it from the popular west side. Viaduct and steam train become an object of cult veneration for the duration of time that the train passes over! It has indeed earned a place among the most famed trains in the world. It is a shame that the navvies who laboriously constructed this line, with its immensely attractive engineering features including its several famed viaducts, cannot be present to reap their hard-earned and thoroughly deserved recognition.

The Lochy is crossed early in the outbound journey and must bow to second place when compared with the other highlights along the route, for in contrast to the aforementioned crowds there was just one other photographer at this location on a Highland morning providing somewhat rare late summer sun. Observant viewers will note that the boiler on this locomotive (and also on that locomotive in use for the second train of the day) unusually faces towards Fort William in contrast to the usual practice of facing Mallaig, thus facilitating those photographers seeking different perspectives. This particular location is often photographed from the west – and into the mid-morning sun.

Near Sandplace, Sunday 19 September 2010: Class 37 37685, operated by West Coast Railways, hauls the 14.55 Liskeard to Looe 'Looe Valley Explorer' special, with GWR Class 9400 0-6-0PT 9466 at the rear in push-mode.

Fulfilling a duty which will deflect *all* interest to the steam locomotive at the rear when on the return journey, it is still unusual for this quiet branch line to entertain main line diesels with traditional carriages in tow. The rolling Cornish countryside will echo the sound of this train for some time after it has passed by, with effort being applied by both the diesel and the steam locomotive judging by the emission of smoke at the back. The East Looe Estuary will very soon come into view and shortly afterwards the scenic harbour of Looe. The small terminus platform may be somewhat overwhelmed by the alighting of all the passengers should they choose to disembark to collect a pasty or ice cream from the nearby shops. They will however have a very limited amount of time to do so, as the steam-hauled charter will soon return up the branch with its by then highly attentive passengers enjoying the sound of steam rather than the English Electric engines of the diesel.

Opposite: Near Terras Crossing, Sunday 19 September 2010: GWR Class 9400 0-6-0PT 9466 approaches with the 15.40 Looe to Liskeard 'Looe Valley Explorer' special.

The local railway photographers were out in force for this very rare occasion when steam visited the Looe Valley branch, which in 2010 was 150 years old. This was all thanks in part to the Looe, Polperro and District Chamber of Trade and Commerce which promoted the concept in conjunction with First Great Western and Vintage Trains. The high tide cooperated when it played its part by filling the estuary with a plentiful swell of seawater just in time for the mid-afternoon return train, though at least it did not cover the road which crosses the estuary at this point (which would have somewhat restricted access and photographic opportunities!). There's a hint of autumn in the trees although the predominant green of summer is still evident in the abundance of leaves which clad the trees overlooking the valley.

Below: Terras Crossing, Sunday 19 September 2010: Class 37 37685 operated by West Coast Railways, approaches with the 17.10 Liskeard to Looe, 'Looe Valley Explorer' special.

It would be interesting to know if the canoeist who is taking advantage of the high tide is aware of the bank of cameras behind him as he paddles his way downstream. He seems oblivious to the various heads looking out from the carriages for the train to halt, sound its horn and then proceed 'growling' across the road and causeway ahead. He may not be aware that such is a very unusual event – although surely he will notice the steam locomotive at the rear? He seems in no rush and is probably enjoying the moment as he gauges the drift of the current and decides how far onwards to go before the tide turns and the marshy land either side of the river emerges, uncovered. Likewise the enthusiasts aboard the train anticipate their return journey behind 9466 as the highlight of their afternoon.

Terras Crossing, Sunday 19 September 2010: GWR Class 9400 0-6-0PT 9466 approaches with the 17.55 Looe to Liskeard 'Looe Valley Explorer'.

No. 9466 was built after the 1948 nationalisation of the post-war railways in 1952 by Robert Stephenson and Hawthorns. Initially allocated to Worcester where it was used for shunting and pilot work, it also worked local passenger and freight trains to Malvern and Evesham and spent its final years in South Wales. Even so, it makes a welcome change to the normal fare of Class 150 and 153 units. Fortunately the line was spared the derided 'Pacer' units which couldn't cope with the sharp curves and 1 in 40 gradient climbing from 130ft (40m) above sea level at Coombe Junction to 328ft (100m) at Liskeard station. Steam locomotives would have worked tender first along the branch and smokebox first when ascending the gradient.

Forder Viaduct, Saturday 20 September 2003: Class 50s, front, 50031 *Hood*; second, 50049 *Defiance*, both in BR blue livery and preserved at the Severn Valley Railway, haul Pathfinder Tours' 'The Cream of Cornwall' 06.40 Slough to Par excursion, passing at midday.

  The author recalls travelling behind paired Class 50s from Bodmin and St Austell to Plymouth on Saturday evenings in the mid-1980s, the sound of which always proved entertaining to listen to. It is likely that the pair at that time normally worked the London sleeper train but on Saturdays when the sleeper was not scheduled they moved only the seated coaching stock to Plymouth, with the second Class 50 included in the formation as an engine movement back to Laira. The Class 50s have proved particularly popular in preservation with no less than eighteen surviving beyond their formal withdrawal from service. As we saw in the photograph of Class 50 50007 *Hercules* at Dawlish (page 8), a few have even been loaned to GB Railfreight on long-term hire, thus being used on the main line in revenue-earning service.

Chapter 3
AUTUMN

Above: Williton, West Somerset Railway, Saturday 23 September 2000: Class 35 'Hymek' D7017 in early BR blue with the 14.50 Minehead to Bishops Lydeard, which appears to be formed of a motley collection of a parcels brake coach, DMU trailers and, at the rear, a BR maroon GUV Parcels van.

The Bristol Channel and Steep Holme Island looming in the mist offer a coastal perspective on the route of the West Somerset Railway at this location, and on clearer days the South Wales coastline is visible. The cows have just returned from milking and the milk lorry will soon be doing its rounds along the Somerset lanes. Fine weather in the latter half of September is always welcome and draws the crowds out to the caravan parks and beaches at Blue Anchor and Minehead. Those using the railway for their trip to the coast will no doubt return to Bishops Lydeard later in the afternoon when a steam locomotive will provide the expected entertainment.

Opposite above: Coombe by Saltash Viaduct, Sunday 26 September 2010: GWR Class 9400 0-6-0PT 9466 at rear of the 09.30 Plymouth to Liskeard, hauled by Class 37/6 37685, operated by West Coast Railways, providing onward steam haulage to Looe with the 'Looe Valley Explorer'.

This seven-span viaduct's height of 86ft (26m) is emphasised at it carries the visiting train above the yachts at anchor. It was first constructed by Brunel who built it on timber piles and used timber trestles instead of stone piers because it crossed a deep, muddy tidal inlet. It was later replaced by a stone viaduct in 1894. The train has previously crossed the Royal Albert Bridge and passed through Saltash station, and will provide a second weekend's opportunity for photographing its journey along the Looe Valley branch line as part of the celebration of the line's 150th anniversary.

Below: Royal Albert Bridge, Sunday 26 September 2010: View from the south-east side.

    This masterpiece of engineering stands like a sentinel guarding a serene stretch of water while presiding over the plethora of almost insignificant motorboats and yachts moored below, in awe at its majestic and haughty tubular tension. Once the tide turns, the River Tamar's current starts to run very fast and catching any reflection is no longer possible. Isambard Kingdom Brunel chose this point 3 miles north-west of Plymouth, where the river narrows, to make the crossing, but even so it is 1,000ft wide and 70ft deep (300m and 21m) at high water here, allowing sufficient height for sailing ships to pass underneath. The bridge is 167ft (51m) above high water mark to the top of the tubes (the Admiralty specified 8ft, 30m mast clearance). It was built by Brunel for the Cornwall Railway while it was leased to the Great Western Railway, and construction began in 1848, it being finally completed in 1859. Brunel, as chief engineer, was first across, but it was to be his last major work – he died three months after the bridge's opening.

Cockwood Harbour, Sunday 26 September 2010: Class A1 4-6-2 60163 *Tornado* crosses the causeway with the 16.42 Kingswear to Bristol return 'Torbay Express'.

This 'new' steam locomotive always turns heads and has won the admiration of those who enjoy the thrill of being hauled by a main line steam locomotive at speed and of course of the hundreds of photographers eager to capture this 'green goddess' at work. It may look like something from a bygone age but it was completed as recently as 2008, built from scratch by a dedicated team of volunteers. *Tornado* is currently limited to 75mph on the main line, but it has always been the intention to run the locomotive at speeds up to 90mph to better fit in with other trains on the busy UK rail network. When undertaking test runs in connection with raising its permitted maximum speed, *Tornado* reached 100mph, a preservation era record, during trials conducted on the East Coast Main Line between Doncaster and Newcastle. The success of this new-build locomotive seems to have inspired a procession long-lost steam locomotive replicas, of various classes.

Between Bodmin General and Boscarne Junction, Bodmin and Wenford Railway, Sunday 10 October 2010: LSWR Class 0298 'Beattie' 2-4-0WT 30587 leads sister locomotive 30585 with the 13.25 Boscarne Junction to Bodmin General.

    These locomotives, of 'Beattie' LSWR design, here seen on a rare pairing during a special event, were of a type built from 1863 to 1875, and were themselves built in 1874. By the end of 1899, after working London suburban passenger services, only the last three 'well tanks' of the class remained, all the others having been withdrawn as they become worn out and redundant. By 1895, both locomotives in this photograph were to be found working the Bodmin and Wadebridge lines with which they ultimately became synonymous. This railway was one of the earliest in Cornwall and was isolated from the main LSWR network until that year. These two locomotives along with one other, 30586, remained in service because of the sharp curves of that railway's freight branch to Wenford Bridge, which carried china clay traffic to the main line, where they were found to be the only suitable engines and worked there for sixty-four years. They were finally withdrawn in 1962 and replaced by GWR 1366 class 0-6-0PT dock tanks when the line came under the control of BR Western Region. No. 30587 was preserved at the Bodmin and Wenford Railway on loan, owned by the National Railway Museum; 30585 is preserved at the Buckinghamshire Railway Centre, owned by the Quainton Railway Society. It was on short-term loan to the Bodmin and Wenford at the time of this picture. T9 30120 was also at this time based at the Bodmin and Wenford.

Opposite: Bodmin General, Bodmin and Wenford Railway, Sunday 10 October 2010: Front, LSWR 0298 'Beattie' 2-4-0WT 30587 awaits watering as also, second in line, 0298 'Beattie' 30585. Rear is LSWR Class T9 4-4-0 30120 awaiting duties .

Here's a rare 'chance' preservation era line-up of LSWR locomotives which might have possibly been seen together at Wadebridge in steam days. Along with the steam, coal dust and grime of the steam shed's environment, this black trio of locomotives exudes atmosphere as does the directed attention by the driver and fireman to the axles and working parts of their locomotive – all these are integral to a working steam railway's essence. T9 30120 had officially returned to traffic at the Bodmin and Wenford Railway on 2 September 2010. The T9 Drummond LSWR express passenger locomotives with their 6ft 7in driving wheels were known as 'Greyhounds' owing to their impressive speeds, achieved in service in their heyday. The shape of these contrasting locomotives may be partly shared, but their duties were very different, with the 'Beattie' locomotives hauling china clay trains whilst the T9s would have been as much at home on expresses on the south-western main line as working passenger trains along the undulating North Cornwall Railway from Okehampton via Halwill to Padstow.

Below: Bodmin, Bodmin and Wenford Railway, Sunday 10 October 2010: GWR 0-6-0PT 5700 Class 4612, running as 4666, approaches Bodmin General near Walker Lines with the 14.25 service from Bodmin Parkway.

This could well be a South Wales branch line location, for the locomotive was based at Neath shed during its final years, or similarly it could be one of the Somerset or Wiltshire rural railways from the years when it was based at Swindon, Chippenham or Bristol. Preservation allows scope for such reminiscences and on occasions a particular locomotive may be a favourite for providing targeted recollections by taking on the identity of another locomotive from the same class. In this case it is sister locomotive 4666 which also spent time in South Wales when it was based at Danygraig, Swansea. No. 4666 also spent time based at nearby Wadebridge shed from 31 December 1959 until 9 February 1963 when it was transferred to Exmouth Junction, and this local interest probably accounts for the reason that 4612 has loaned its true identity.

Berwyn, Llangollen Railway, Saturday 13 October 2001: Class 46 46010 arrives with the 12.00 from Llangollen to Carrog.

This train is seen running alongside the River Dee and passing Berwyn station's half-timbered Tudor style building, designed to match the adjacent Chain Bridge Hotel just across the river. The 1920s chain bridge provided easy access for guests arriving by train to the picturesque location's hotel. While the line would not have not carried 'Peak' class diesel locomotives, the scenery is certainly reminiscent of the Peak District, and we could well be in Monsal Dale and viewing a Midland Railway scene in the late 1960s alongside the River Wye – for both railway routes share a limestone geology. In the latter case the train would be heading for either London St Pancras or Manchester Central. The autumn mist adds atmosphere to accompany the salute provided by this powerful locomotive.

Glyndyfrdwy, Llangollen Railway, Saturday 13 October 2001: Class 46 46010 passes alongside the River Dee with the 12.48 Carrog to Llangollen.

The mellow autumn colours in this tranquil pastoral scene provide an appropriate hue in which to pay tribute to the 'Peak' class locomotive wending its way alongside the River Dee. Very little would date the photograph as belonging to the preservation era, and we could well be viewing a genuine 'Peak' hauled main line service from the 1970s passing through Millers Dale in the Peak District, here caught in the welcome time warp that the preserved railways can provide. The BR blue certainly suited the Class 45 and 46 locomotives as much as did the earlier BR green and any debate about such is usually weighted by the fact that BR policy meant that virtually every locomotive bore the same blue and yellow!

Above: Victoria Bridge, Severn Valley Railway, Saturday 13 October 1990: Class 55 'Deltic' D9000 55022 *Royal Scots Grey* with the 14.55 Bridgnorth to Kidderminster.

The Severn Valley and the railway which threads its way alongside is particularly attractive in the autumn gold hues of the many trees which line its banks. The two-tone British Railways green worn by *Royal Scots Grey* certainly has a chance to gleam and impress when contrasted with the display of colours provided by nature. The metallic green of the cast-iron arched bridge also bears witness to its ironwork manufacturers whose name is proudly displayed on the metalwork as that 'cast and erected by the Coalbrookdale Company', built 1861, and opened for traffic on 31 January 1862. Its span of 200ft (61m), was the longest single-span bridge made of cast iron in Britain when built. In preservation, major refurbishment was carried out during the winters of 1979–80, and 2003–04. A permanent speed limit of 15mph applies to all trains crossing the bridge and operating restrictions mean that two large engines may not work double-headed over it.

Opposite above: Near Foley Park, Severn Valley Railway, Saturday 15 October 2005: Class 73 E6006 hauls the 14.10 Bewdley to Kidderminster 'shuttle'.

The versatile electro diesels working in main line service feature in other photographs in this book. Here's one of the many preserved Class 73s, intriguingly in truly Great Western territory, but that simply illustrates the point that they still have an active life beyond their once strictly observed Southern Region boundaries. The early electric blue livery, with the grey stripe and lower yellow cab ends, looks reminiscent of that applied to the Class 85 West Coast Main Line overhead electric locomotives. Maybe the nearest equivalent livery in the modern railway scene as applied to Class 73s is that worn by the small fleet which are adorned with the 'Caledonian Sleeper' livery, even if its colour description is 'Midnight Teal'. These dedicated locomotives have been significantly rebuilt, including the incorporation of their 1600hp MTU 'R43 4000' V8 diesel engines.

Below: Near Foley Park, Severn Valley Railway, Saturday 15 October 2005: FM Rail Fragonset Class 47/7 47712 *Artemis* hauls the 15.45 Kidderminster to Bewdley.

Seen in Fragonset black livery, this was one of four Class 47/7 locomotives which were purchased by Fragonset Railways in the company's early days. The appearance of Fragonset Railways on the railway scene during 1997 as a spot hire company introduced a new livery and operator. They quickly drew interest from railway photographers and those wishing haulage by locomotive, especially when in 1998 the company purchased several redundant Class 31 locomotives from EWS. They saw service on Silverlink services on the Marston Vale Line, operating in top and tail mode with two carriages. No. 47712 saw further service with DRS and currently resides with Locomotive Services Limited on hire from the Crewe Diesel Preservation Group.

Above: Lostwithiel, Thursday 15 October 2020: Great Western 'Castle' HST set passes with the 14.46 Plymouth to Penzance.

A reminder of our railway heritage is strongly represented here, with the signal box, semaphore signals, HST power car and chequered flag stone platform surface. Such scenes tend to be found far from busy suburban routes and main lines, which are understandably given higher priority for modernisation. The recently-introduced 'Castle' train formations are a boon to this area and provide very much improved accommodation – upgraded HST coaching stock – compared to the previous Class 150 'Sprinters', usually only two-car, which dominated the services now taken over by this fleet of trains. A journey all the way from Bristol to Penzance on the 'Sprinters' must have been something of an endurance test!

Opposite above: Restormal, Thursday 15 October 2020: A pair of Great Western Class 158s pass with the 15.15 Penzance to Plymouth.

In the same way as the 'Castle' sets have upgraded the travel experience of passengers in Cornwall, so also have the Class 158s which have started to spread their wings over the Cornish main line and Barnstaple branches, having been cascaded down from the Bristol and Wessex areas, which in turn have inherited Thames Turbo stock. This pairing of units seems a generous offering for a midweek mid-afternoon service but that may have something to do with the need to offer greater space for social distancing as a safety measure during the pandemic. There's a gentle warmth in the afternoon sun but the onset of autumnal hues is starting to show and soon the cooler climate of the autumn will become established – the evenings are already noticeably shorter, and the lengthening shadows are present even at this stage of the day.

Below: Near Bicknoller, West Somerset Railway, Saturday 23 October 2010: GWR 2-6-2T 5101 Class 4160 hauls the 14.25 Bishops Lydeard to Minehead.

Sunshine highlights the Quantocks' trees in their transition from green to golden hues and the ferns are turning to russet brown. Sheep graze on the rich green Somerset grass and, unseen, birds of prey are busy scanning for their next meal. The authentic green of the Great Western locomotive is complemented by the chocolate and cream of the carriages in a scene which could so easily pass for a genuine 1950s West Country rural image. The lineside hut adds a further hint of persuasion that this is the reality. It's the first weekend of the school October half-term holidays and this train is likely to be fairly quiet as many people will be still on their journeys down to the South West. Six carriages is the regular length for busy seasons and certainly the railway can expect a promising week of busy trains, especially when the weather is less favourable.

Oxted, Sunday 24 October 2010: Southern Class 377 'Electrostar' EMU 377140 departs with the 10.08 service to London Victoria, ex-East Grinstead.

This pleasant location at the foot of the North Downs reminds us of the fine scenery afforded to travellers in this area of rural Surrey. EMUs tend to receive less photographic attention than locomotives, despite the fact that the era of Southern green adorning vintage electric trains working alongside Southern Region steam in the 1960s is one of the more interesting aspects of our rich railway tapestry. The design of the 'Electrostar' units is aesthetically appealing as it avoids the rather box-like designs of the 1980s' and 90s' fleets of new generation electric units serving the third rail territory of South London and Surrey. The colourful Southern livery is functional and yet striking in its sleek lines which enhance the curvature of the carriages, especially when kept in such sparkling clean condition as here.

Horsted Keynes, Bluebell Railway, Sunday 24 October 2010: Southern Railway Class E4 0-6-2T 32473 *Birch Grove* arrives with a mid-morning service from Sheffield Park.

The cool autumnal air enhances the steam exhaust trail emitted from *Birch Grove*'s chimney as it completes its climb into Horsted Keynes. The Southern green livery well matches those vintage carriages, the first of which is a 1922-built third-class SECR (South East & Chatham Railway) 'hundred seater' which carried London commuters, several of which were still in daily use in 1960 forming part of coaching sets on services from Tunbridge Wells West, Forest Row and East Grinstead into and out of London Bridge. Next to it is a Southern Railway Maunsell third, one of a type used from 1930 in conjunction with kitchen dining cars to providing dining accommodation on prestigious trains such as the 'Bournemouth Limited', and on services between London Waterloo and Portsmouth, Exeter or Weymouth.

Above: Horsted Keynes, Bluebell Railway, Sunday 24 October 2010: Front, SECR Class P 0-6-0T 31178; second, SECR Class C 0-6-0 31592 with the 11.33 service from Horsted Keynes to Sheffield Park.

Autumnal trees salute these magnificent vintage locomotives, both of Wainwright design, seen here proudly showing off their elegant features complimented by immaculate SECR paintwork as highlighted by the morning sunlight. The 'full Wainwright' lined green livery for SECR locomotives, beautifully finished with complex lining and burnished brass dome covers, was one of the most elaborate and decorative to be seen in the UK. No. 31178 celebrated its centenary during this year, for it was built at Ashford works in 1910. It worked push-pull services in south-east London and spent several years operating over the Westerham branch while based at Tonbridge. It later saw use on shunting duties around the docks of Folkestone and Dover where it shunted the town yard, the ferry dock and the harbour board lines. Its more elderly partner 31592 was built in 1902 at the London, Chatham and Dover Railway Longhedge Works at Battersea. SECR Class C locomotives were used on semi-fast passenger trains as well as a great variety of goods trains. They also saw use on occasional passenger excursion trains (such as hop-picking specials). This was the largest of the 0-6-0 classes to be found on the Southern, with locomotives being allocated to many sheds for working on mixed traffic duties. No. 31592 gave much of its post-nationalisation service while based at Ramsgate, Tonbridge and Ashford.

Opposite above: Horsted Keynes, Bluebell Railway, Sunday 24 October 2010: Front, SECR Class P 0-6-0T 31178; second, SECR Class C 0-6-0 31592 with the 11.33 service from Horsted Keynes to Sheffield Park.

These immaculate statesman-like locomotives are appropriately seen hauling a directors' saloon no. 706E, LNER 43909, which was built for the Great Northern Railway in 1897. For a rare chance to ride in this pristine vintage clerestory saloon, on this special occasion behind this graceful duo, it is available for first-class ticket holders on a number of weekends each year as well as for private hire. It remained in use for the GNR/LNER directors, then for the British Railways Eastern Region general manager until 1969, when it was withdrawn. As one of the last remaining privately owned coaches on the Bluebell, the saloon's dedicated team of owners and friends, the Howlden Trust (so named after E.F. Howlden, the saloon's designer), have given their devoted time and effort to restoring the saloon to its GNR/LNER appearance.

Below: Horsted Keynes, Bluebell Railway, Sunday 24 October 2010: LSWR Class N15 'King Arthur' 4-6-0 30777 *Sir Lamiel* departs with the 12.10 to Kingscote.

Photographers line up in tribute to this fine Maunsell locomotive dating from 1925, which is a Southern Railway development of the LSWR design which originated in 1918 at the end of the First World War, when Robert Urie, then chief mechanical engineer of the Southern Railway, introduced these locomotives. It was one of the batch of thirty engines built at the North British Locomotive Works in Glasgow. Smoke deflectors were fitted in December 1927. The class was given names associated with the West Country and the legend of King Arthur and the knights of the Round Table, one of whom was Sir Lamiel of Cardiff. It would have been seen working expresses from Waterloo to Salisbury and Exeter and also Bournemouth. During its working life it carried a number of liveries in addition to its original Southern Railway olive green, as seen here. *Sir Lamiel* was withdrawn from service in October 1961 after a relatively short working life of some thirty-six years. This was owing to the British Railways Modernisation Plan of 1955 which quickly introduced the use of diesels and therefore led to the consequent early withdrawal of steam engines, many of which were fit for further years of service.

Above: Horsted Keynes, Bluebell Railway, Sunday 24 October 2010: Front, SECR Class P 0-6-0T 31178; second, SECR Class C 0-6-0 31592 arrive with an early afternoon service from Sheffield Park, 12.45 onwards to Kingscote.

One might be tempted to caption this as 'Little and Large' although 31178 as the smaller of the two engines appears to be doing most of the work here. Meanwhile the rich grass of the Sussex meadow seems the star attraction for the cows, whose milk must inevitably be transported by road tanker rather than by one of the milk trains that were integral to the era of steam trains. Might 31592 have hauled such a train in its heyday? The weather is perfect and the cool air plays its part too in allowing the pair forming the real star attraction to make their very best impression on passengers and photographers alike. Railway companies expressed their importance, pride and elegance through the liveries applied to their locomotives and coaching stock, and some of those applied during the late Victorian era suggest that such an ostentatious adornment was almost expected, certainly approved of and admired by the general public and train enthusiasts. Certain, though not all, modern era liveries could learn much from this colourful aspect of our railway history.

Opposite above: Horsted Keynes, Bluebell Railway, Sunday 24 October 2010: LBSCR Class A1X 'Terrier' 0-6-0T 32655 *Stepney* provides local brake van rides, early afternoon.

It is interesting to note that a named Class A1 Stroudley design locomotive is here being used for a short shuttle journey, in a similar way to that we which we saw 32662 *Martello* performing at Corfe Common on the Swanage Railway (page 120), although this time with brake vans containing the contented passengers. This underlines these locomotives' continued popularity in the heritage era just as much as in their heyday of every day service. 'Giants of Steam' (the theme of this special event) have their own appeal but, rather like small steam boats or paddle steamers on Britain's lakes or narrow-bodied buses cruising the lanes of South Devon during the Kingsbridge bus rally, 'small' has its own appeal. Perhaps the local train with a small engine making a reliable regular appearance at a village station along a branch line was something the general public could relate to at a personal level, in comparison to the gleaming bulky mainline steeds speeding between cities and towns across the UK.

Below: Horsted Keynes, Bluebell Railway, Sunday 24 October 2010: right, LBSCR Class A1X 'Terrier' 0-6-0T 32655 *Stepney* provides local brake van rides, early afternoon; left, Southern Railway Class U 2-6-0 31638 departs with the 13.20 to Kingscote.

The combined splendour of shadows and steam, accompanied by a cacophony of hissing and puffing as both locomotives strive to express their very essence, must surely echo to the delight of onlookers and passengers alike, almost drawing them into a stupor from such a sensation. It's a marvellous time capsule and the Bluebell Railway deserves full praise for being able to recreate this sort of scene with its authentic capture of the heart of the steam era on the Southern Railway. We could well be backtracked to 31638's time plying its traditional territory somewhere along the Portsmouth or Brighton main lines, or on the Salisbury to Southampton line. Maybe we can take a clue from locomotives in the distant yard, where we can just see the front of Southern Railway 'West Country' Bulleid design 4-6-2 34023 *Blackmore Vale*.

Horsted House Bridge, Bluebell Railway, Sunday 24 October 2010: A mid-afternoon service to Sheffield Park from Kingscote nears Horsted Keynes with, front, SECR Class P 0-6-0T 31178; second, SECR Class C 0-6-0 31592.

The dappled autumnal sunlight interweaving the multitude of shadows cast by the encroaching trees, still in full leaf, pays tribute to Wainwright's fine design detail demonstrated in these characterful engines appearing as guests and contributing their own brand of green as part of the scene's quilted pattern of colours. The gentle light also highlights the smart teak panelling of the directors' saloon. Interestingly this carriage appeared in the film *The Railway Children* conveying the elderly director of the railway, who waved at the children from the carriage window and helped when their mother became sick. The interior contains two luxurious saloons, one of which is laid out in lounge style, the other in boardroom style. Such luxury was deemed appropriate for railway company directors who presumably must accept first class as the best on offer in our modern times.

Horsted Keynes, Bluebell Railway, Sunday 24 October 2010: Front, LSWR Class N15 'King Arthur' 4-6-0 30777 *Sir Lamiel*; second, Southern Railway 'Battle of Britain' Class 4-6-2 34059 *Sir Archibald Sinclair* approach with the 16.40 Horsted Keynes to Kingscote.

Creating a truly autumnal atmosphere while emitting a crescendo of steam and sound , these 'Giants of Steam' really impress with their glistening paintwork reflecting the receding golden rays of the sun and the onset of cooler late-afternoon air highlights their steam trail. Along with the Southern green of the carriages, the light reveals the pinnacle of Southern steam locomotive design as evidenced during the 1950s British Railways era. No. 30777 *Sir Lamiel* was based at Nine Elms, Stewarts Lane and Dover Marine during 1951,whereas 34059 *Sir Archibald Sinclair* was based at Nine Elms until it moved on to Exmouth Junction in March 1951, so this exact pairing would not have occurred but it's still a reminder of the power and prestige expressed by the larger engines that ruled over the main lines of Southern England during the halcyon days of steam.

Above: Horsted Keynes, Bluebell Railway, Sunday 24 October 2010: Southern Railway Class U 2-6-0 31638 departs with a late afternoon Pullman dining train to Sheffield Park.

The golden hues of the setting sun highlight the Pullman cream and brown livery of the carriages in which the epitome of traditional luxury was provided as the optimum form of rail travel, in first-class coaches with a steward service. The leading Pullman carriage, named *Fingall*, was the first of the Bluebell Railway's four Pullmans to be acquired. It is a Pullman kitchen first, built by the Birmingham Railway Carriage and Wagon Co. in 1924 for the Yorkshire Pullman. It was put to use on the 'White Pullman' which, in 1929, was named the 'Golden Arrow'. Post war, it saw further use on the Southern Region, including the 'Bournemouth Belle'. The equally interesting vehicle immediately behind the locomotive is a 1938-built London Midland and Scottish Railway (LMS) six-wheel gangwayed luggage/guard's brake van. The guard's area has been partitioned off, and the remainder of the interior fitted out to provide the pantry and service needs for the Bluebell's Pullman train. It has been painted in Pullman colours to blend in with the remainder of the Pullman set (and its roof has subsequently been painted white).

Opposite above: Roebuck Farm, West Somerset Railway, Saturday 25 October 2003: Class 117 Pressed Steel DMU operates the 16.55 Bishops Lydeard to Minehead.

A threatening sky in the background suggests a shower over the Quantocks but the photographer has the benefit of the late afternoon sun to draw out the autumnal colours now becoming vivid in their intensity. The BR green of the diesel unit offers an interesting contrast to the variety of hues in the foliage and grasses of the meadow. At this time of year, passenger numbers travelling on the last trains of the day will be subdued and a three-carriage set will prove more than adequate for the purpose. Some preserved railways have invested in purchasing 'Pacer' units to meet similar demand but travelling in one along 20 miles, the full length of this railway, the shaking and bouncing of those riding on board may deter rather than encourage any future return.

Below: Near Bicknoller, West Somerset Railway, 25 October 2003: Class 117 Pressed Steel DMU operates the 13.35 Minehead to Bishops Lydeard.

The 'speed whiskers' applied to the early BR green diesel multiple units did offer a relief to their appearance at a time when, for steam enthusiasts, their introduction replaced the time-honoured appearance of the branch line steam train wending its way through the countryside. Modern, warm and business-like, they offered a sturdy and decent ride. The Pressed Steel units rolled around far less than the Cravens-built DMUs which offered the equivalent of a ride on Blackpool fair's roller coaster when hitting any undulations in the track at speed or even just following the contours of the hills and curves of the branches where they operated. They were certainly slow to accelerate in comparison to the second generation diesel units but they could pick up quite a speed; passing through wayside stations in these at 70mph was an enlivening experience.

Pulborough, Monday 25 October 2010: Southern Class 377/4 'Electrostar' EMU 377416 approaches with the 10.51 service to Bognor Regis, 09.32 ex-London Victoria.

A crisp autumn morning with its low sun and lengthening shadows sees the approaching train greeted by golden hues in leaves that, once they fall, will require the attention of the railhead treatment trains that provide daily remedial action to the slippery mulch which causes wheel flats and other difficulties at this time of year. The semaphore signals here remained until early 2014, from when control was transferred to Three Bridges. Bognor and Littlehampton retain semaphores.

Opposite below: Pulborough, Monday 25 October 2010: Southern Class 377/4 'Electrostar' EMU 377421 departs with the 10.55 service to London Victoria, 10.30 ex-Bognor Regis. The photograph shows the island platform for the up line with the far side no doubt previously serving the Midhurst branch trains.

Pulborough station stands on the Three Bridges/Arundel railway line. It was first opened on 10 October 1859 and progressively grew with additional traffic deriving from a branch line to Midhurst via Petworth that was opened in 1866. The present Pulbrough signal box, a Saxby & Farmer Type 5 design, was built in 1878. The closure of the Midhurst branch line, due to a growth in competition with road traffic, resulted in the closure of the goods yards during the mid-1960s; however, the volume of passenger traffic has ensured that the signal box, a Grade II listed building, has remained in operation.

Below: Pulborough, Monday 25 October 2010: Southern Class 377 'Electrostar' EMU 377117 approaches the station from the south, passing autumnal-coloured beech trees with the 11.12 Portsmouth Harbour 'fast' service to Horsham (where it would attach to another unit for onward journey to London Victoria).

Here's a pleasant vista with the South Downs in the distance. The trees seem to salute the passing train with its colourful livery enhanced by the low sunlight. The 'Electrostar' units have benefitted from refurbishment under Govia Thameslink Railway's fleet modernisation programme. The £55m programme known as 'Project Aurora' covers 214 Bombardier Transportation Class 377 'Electrostar' sets operated on Southern services, and 56 similar Class 387 units used on Gatwick Express and Great Northern services. The work is undertaken at GTR's Selhurst depot. Performance monitoring and fault diagnosis systems, including a 'smart' on-train data recorder, will predict and diagnose faults to help reduce the time when vehicles are out of service for maintenance or repair.

Above: Amberley, Arun river bridge, Monday 25 October 2010: Southern Class 377 'Electrostar' EMU approaches with the 14.00 Horsham (13.02 ex-London Victoria) to Portsmouth Harbour.

An idyllic view over the meadows and pastures of this Sussex landscape, with the swans busily engaged in preening and feeding, entirely oblivious to the passing trains crossing the River Arun. Gentle sunshine pays tribute to those mellow days of early autumn which fade in our memory as winter approaches. It's one of those few warm late October days when everything in nature conspires to be at its most serene before the onset of shorter days, gales and rain that will inevitably follow in the near future. The rustic gateway beckons us to make the best of the countryside during this window of opportunity.

Opposite above: Conwy Castle and Conwy Estuary, Thursday 26 October 2000: EWS Class 37/7 37893 hauls 12.07 Birmingham New St to Holyhead – one of the last diagrams for loco-hauled North Wales Coast trains.

The train departs Robert Stephenson's tubular railway bridge and is immediately overwhelmed by the compact and formidable castle which dates back to 1283 when construction started. Conwy Castle and town are surrounded by a well-preserved town wall, as can be seen on the left. This helps the town maintain a medieval character lost by some other Welsh castle towns over the years. Its eight great towers are all intact, from one of which flutter the Welsh flags in the westerly breeze. These towers afford spectacular views over the town, surrounding coastline and countryside. Yachts and small motor boats are safely protected by the shelter offered by the quay and harbour.

Below: Newby Bridge, Lakeside and Haverthwaite Railway, Thursday 26 October 2006: Class 4MT 2-6-4T 42073 hauls 15.45 Lakeside to Haverthwaite.

   The gentle light of a mid-autumn day illuminates the picturesque rolling fells of lowland Lakeland, and the Lakeland stone provides a gentle hue of warmth in the farm buildings and bridge crossing the line. It's not too cool to enjoy a trip by boat on the lake from Lakeside Pier station situated at the south end of Lake Windermere. The vista of the Lakeland mountains opens up spectacularly to reward passengers on their arrival at the terminus. The illustrated setting is well suited to this locomotive which first saw service on the Southern Region, having been built at Brighton and entered service in 1950. In 1957 its duties transferred to Yorkshire where it worked from Bradford Hammerton Street and Sowerby Bridge, and a year later from York and Leeds Neville Hill. It's work along the Lakeside and Haverthwaite Railway will not prove too taxing, giving the crew time to enjoy the autumnal colours and lapping waters of the lake alongside which it runs for a short time.

Weybourne, North Norfolk Railway, Friday 26 October 2007: Metro-Cammell Class 101 DMU 56062 and 51228 arriving with the 15.00 Holt to Sheringham.

Here's a scene that could undoubtedly be straight from any rural branch line in Norfolk during the early 1970s, and the destination blind reveals Thetford as complicit in this reminiscence. The morning's fog has lifted to a give a cloudy day, yet with enough brightness to allow the shadows from the trees to fall on the nearby fields. Interestingly the semaphore signals at Weybourne are lower quadrant – usually a feature of the Great Western. The driver conveys the token ready to pass over to the signalman. Such DMUs were taken for granted during their years of service and yet they form an invaluable part of the preservation scene in modern times as demonstrated by their presence on most preservation railways – a tribute to their humble if mundane role in the realms of railway history. When several were joined together to reinforce rush-hour or summer Saturday services to the coast, they could provide an impressive picture.

East Combe, West Somerset Railway, Sunday 26 October 2008: Derby Suburban Class 115 passes, forming the 12.10 Bishops Lydeard to Crowcombe service.

The gateway leads to a ploughed field composed of the red soils of West Somerset, which are complemented by the red hues of the maple tree on the left. It's a scene which suggests autumn has definitely arrived, along with the showers of typical of late October which make the soils appear somewhat muddy. The diesel unit conveys a sense of purpose as it descends towards Crowcombe on a local service. A break in the heavy cloud over the Quantocks suggests that brighter weather may follow, especially nearer the coastline towards which later trains to Minehead will journey.

East Combe, West Somerset Railway, Sunday 26 October 2008: 4-6-2 West Country 'Pacific' 34046 *Braunton* with the 14.25 Bishops Lydeard to Minehead.

Braunton was initially allocated to Exmouth Junction shed and consequently it would have been seen on the Barnstaple to Ilfracombe line passing through the town of Braunton, after which it was later named. The steep gradient out of Ilfracombe would have provided it with plenty of opportunity for capacious smoke and a cacophony of sound. Later based at Salisbury, Brighton and Bournemouth locomotive sheds , it spent much time hauling express trains from London Waterloo to Weymouth and also at much lower speeds on the more curvaceous and hilly route of the Somerset and Dorset line between Bath and Bournemouth. During the locomotive's career it hauled many prestigious named trains such as the 'Atlantic Coast Express' and the 'Pines Express'. On the West Somerset Railway, a lengthy restoration by the heritage engineering centre at Williton station transformed *Braunton* from rusty hulk to a 1940s engineering marvel and its release to traffic in September 2008 was met with fully deserved adulation and applause.

Castle Hill, West Somerset Railway, Sunday 26 October 2008: Front, GWR 2-6-2T 5101 Class 4160; second, GWR 0-6-2T 5600 Class 6695, hauling 14.20 Minehead to Bishops Lydeard.

    The cooler autumn air means that the exhaust proves much more evident and helps to provide a sense of movement and expression which is much harder to capture on camera during the warm summer months. Preserved railways tend to promote steam gala events during the spring and early summer. This means they can concentrate on carrying the more generally interested public during the midsummer vacation using an enhanced timetable to accommodate the increased numbers of day trippers who choose to travel behind a steam engine. If the weather is nice and sunny and there's a beach nearby, families will avoid the railway and travel on the cloudier or wet days that the British summer usually bestows. The West Somerset Railway has the additional advantage, rather like the Paignton and Dartmouth Steam Railway, of passing by small resorts with beaches and reaching a seaside town with all-weather amenities. Other preserved railways need to provide themed events and joint admission tickets with nearby local attractions to encourage people to come and travel.

Blue Anchor, West Somerset Railway, Sunday 26 October 2008: 4-6-2 West Country 'Pacific' 34046 *Braunton*, with the 14.25 Bishops Lydeard to Minehead.

   The cooler autumn air appears to merge the steam with the clouds that have built up over the land. The cliffs by West Quantoxshead dip down to the cool waters of the Bristol Channel, which laps the beach at Blue Anchor. The location is a favourite for photographers as trains draw out of the station to run alongside the coast before heading a little inland for Dunster. Those walking along the shore can't fail to notice the steam trains passing and will hopefully be tempted to try out a ride on the line. At the end of October daylight hours become even shorter, as the clocks revert to Greenwich Mean Time (GMT) after the end of the period known as British Summer Time (BST). It is interesting to note that GMT was adopted across Great Britain by the Railway Clearing House in December 1847. With the introduction of the railways, travel became faster. With every station keeping its own local mean time, the need for a synchronised time arose. The first railway company to implement a common time for all stations, appropriately named 'Railway Time', was the Great Western Railway in November 1840. By 1847, most railways were using 'London Time': time set at the Royal Observatory in Greenwich.

East Combe, West Somerset Railway, Sunday 26 October 2008: 'Warship' Class 42 D832 *Onslaught*, preserved on the East Lancs Railway, hauls the 15.20 Minehead to Bishops Lydeard.

In the mid-1960s the Western Region decided on maroon as its new house colour for main line diesel locomotives, this going very much against standard schemes imposed by BR's overall management. The Western Region maroon livery set apart the 'Western' and 'Warship' locomotives from diesel locomotives of other regions. Half yellow nose ends appeared from January 1962 and eventually several maroon 'Warships' were among those which, along with all BR blue-liveried locomotives, received full yellow ends. A small number of maroon liveried 'Warships' including D809, D815 and D817 remained in traffic until 5 October 1971. The summer of 1959 saw 100mph service trains diagrammed for D800s, with the Paddington to Bristol 'Bristolian' express set a schedule of 100 minutes. Following a much more relaxed schedule here, the locomotive's maroon livery blends in particularly well with the red soil of the recently ploughed field and the full yellow end offers a useful contrast.

Yeoford, Saturday 30 October 2010: First Great Western Class 153 153329 at the rear of a Class 142 departs on the 11.53 Exmouth/12.27 Exeter St Davids to Barnstaple.

A colourful late October floral display nicely matches the colours of the departing diesel unit. The 'Tarka Line Flowers Competition' has been an annual event for much of the past decade. Each station along the line would be invited to take part and volunteers have helped to carry out the planting and tending of the flowers. The aim has been to make the stations, all of which (except Barnstaple) are unstaffed, as attractive as possible for the enjoyment of passengers. First Great Western assisted in providing generous sponsorship. Yeoford was the overall winner in 2010 and received the Tarka Rail Association Rose Bowl and a certificate, together with complimentary train tickets from First Great Western.

On the left is the still-extant down platform once used by previous Okehampton branch line services, with the passenger service from Exeter to that town finally withdrawn on 5 June 1972. Until very recently this station has been bypassed by only the Okehampton summer Sundays DMU service whereas a two hourly weekday service has been introduced from mid-November 2021. In the waiting room on the right, locals have set up a free lending library on the platform still in use. As this station is only a request halt, it's probably best not to get too absorbed in the book you borrow to browse through, lest your train driver doesn't think you want to stop the train!

Above and below: Yeoford, Saturday 30 October 2010, views north and south: A pair of First Great Western Class 142s with, front, 142068; rear, 142064 (both in North Western Trains livery), are seen arriving and paused at the station with a very well patronised 12.43 Barnstaple to Exmouth, presumably with Saturday shoppers heading for Exeter city centre.

The typical rolling hills and steep valleys enfolding babbling brooks and gurgling streams, along with their prominent churches in this scenic part of Devon, reflect the dispersed nature of the various villages and hamlets that are linked by typical high-hedged Devon lanes. The railway to Barnstaple actually passes close to the village of Colebrooke where St Andrews Church with its fifteenth-century tower can be seen in the background. Its nearest station would actually have been on the Okehampton route, though it never was served by a local station. As also seen in the previous photograph, the Yeoford down platform still exists but excessive costs involved are considered too much to reintroduce its use to passengers despite the fact that the Okehampton branch has now been upgraded for its new two-hourly service. The North Western Trains livery betrays the original suburban area that these 'Pacers' would have traversed, but their use on a lengthy rural branch line must have provided a lively ride to endure if travelling the full length to and from Barnstaple.

Above: Tavistock Junction, Wednesday 31 October 1990: Class 50 50046 *Ajax* arrives mid-afternoon with a ballast train and passes stabled ECC china clay wagons

A reminder that in their later days, the Class 50 locomotives could be found working such trains as this – a far cry from their express passenger role that earned them such favour from the rail enthusiast fraternity. The BR large logo blue livery has become begrimed, and it all hints that this locomotive was in its own autumn at the time of this photograph, being withdrawn in March 1992. Even so, when you consider that it justifies a brand new powerful Class 70 locomotive dedicated to this type of work to handle the heavy loads of ballast, that's an accolade in itself for a Class 50 to be hauling this type of train in its final years. They were certainly capable of hauling the equally heavy china clay wagons seen here on the right. These were conveyed by a Class 08 diesel shunter from Tavistock Junction to the dries at Marsh Mills. The site was taken over by Imerys in 1999.

Opposite above: Ocean Sidings, Laira, Plymouth, Friday 2 November 1990: An unidentified Class 47/4 in charge of the 14.28 Plymouth to Newcastle parcels passes, from left to right, withdrawn Class 50 locomotives, (most with nameplates removed) 50021 *Rodney*, 50016 *Barham*, 50020 *Revenge*, 50040 *Centurion*, 50050 *Fearless*, 50004 *St Vincent* and 50035 *Ark Royal*.

Another parallel with our look at the season of autumn: these Class 50s are, like the autumn leaves, literally into their very final days, at least in ordinary working service. No. 50050 *Fearless* was one of the two class members that worked the final railtour, 'The 50 Terminator', in March 1994. The tour went from London Waterloo to Penzance and back into London Paddington.

Of the withdrawn assemblage seen here, 50021 *Rodney*, 50050 *Fearless* and 50035 *Ark Royal* reached preservation rather than the cutter's torch.

Below: Dartington, South Devon Railway, Saturday 4 November 2006: Class 20 D8110/20110 is operating the 14.30 from Buckfastleigh to Totnes. Preserved at the South Devon Railway at that time.

Looking bristling in the early afternoon sunshine, the smart BR blue Class 20 is paraded by the golden hues of the leaves turning from lush green to amber then red, and their sequence of natural colour change is almost an uncanny mirror of railway signalling colours. The mirrored reflection is also very impressive and suggests there has been no recent rain to swell the River Dart as often happens at this time in autumn. The Scottie dog is a reminder that this Class 20 was first allocated to Glasgow's Eastfield Depot. Class 20s worked nose-first individually in their early years, and were later paired up nose to nose to eliminate the single cab issue. Running them in pairs also meant that, with the combined power of 200 hp they were able to haul the heavier block freight trains with which they became associated.

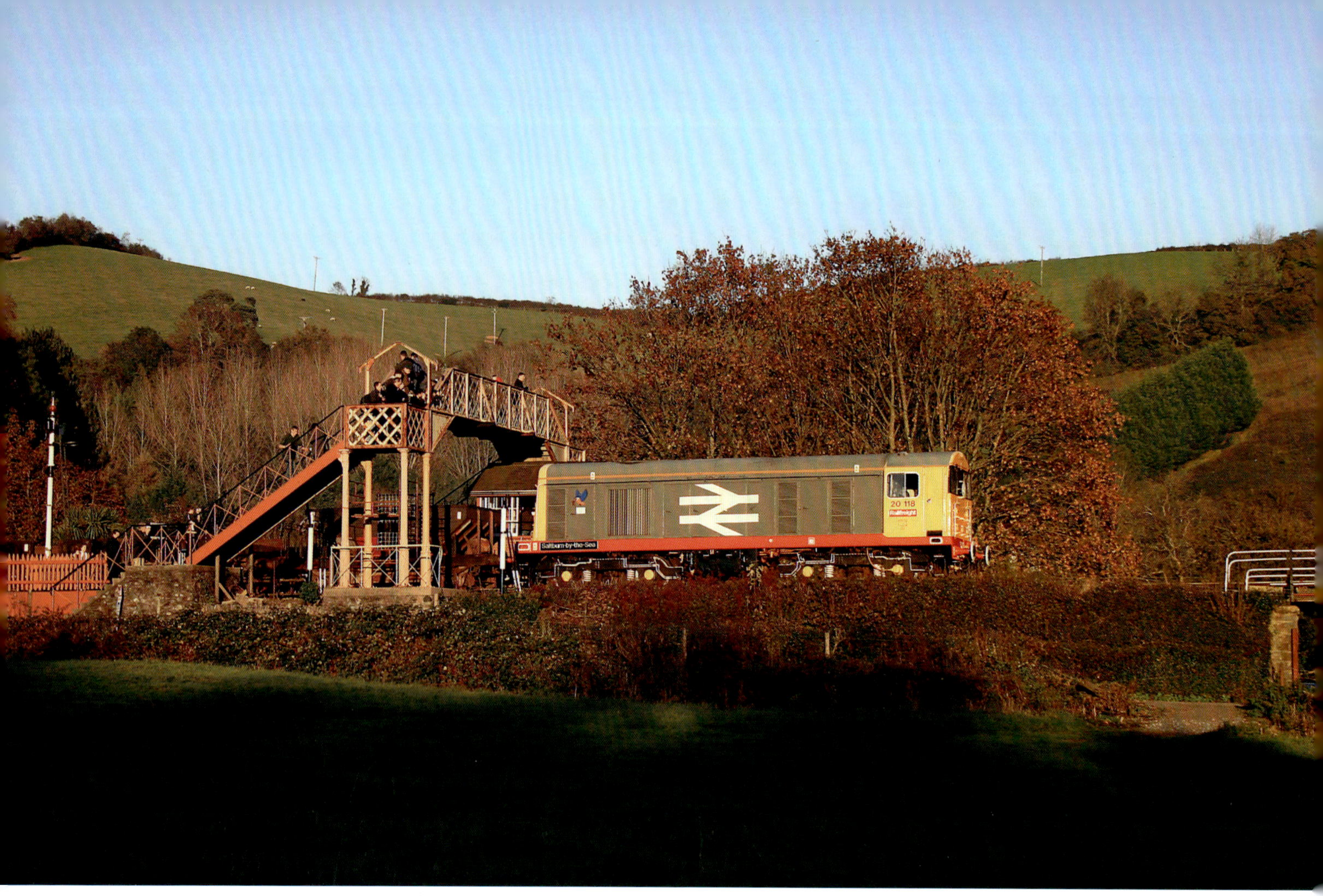
20 118
Railfreight
Saltburn-by-the-Sea

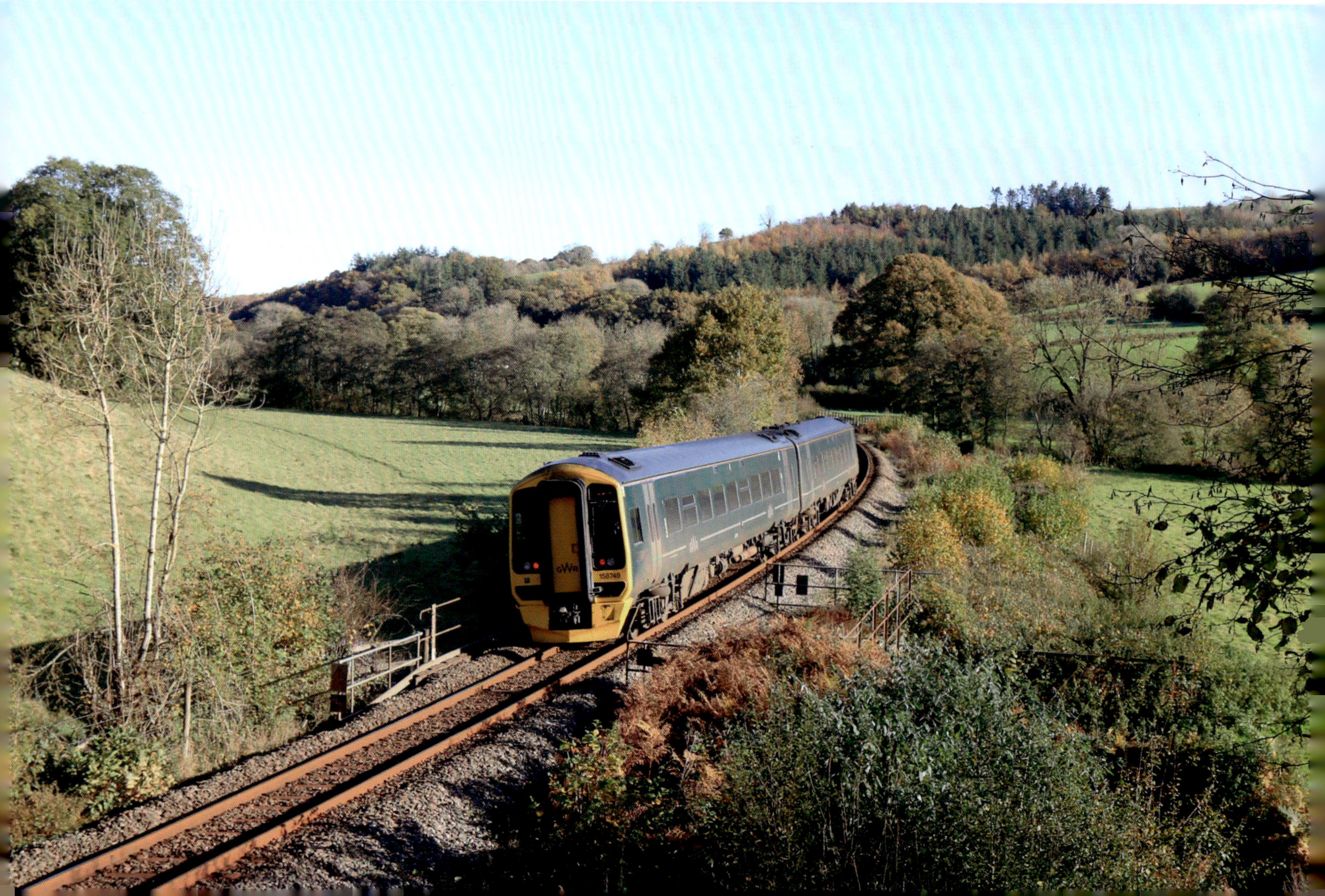
GWR
158749

Opposite above: Buckfastleigh, South Devon Railway, Saturday 4 November 2006: Class 20 D8118 20118 departs with the 15.53 ballast to Bishop's Bridge.

Preservation can recreate some very evocative scenes such as this. The station footbridge, with its lattice metalwork, signal box, semaphore signal and traditional fencing combine to suggest authenticity while the livery provided for the veteran Class 20 in Railfreight grey livery with wrap-around yellow ends reminds us of the era which saw the implementation of the operating sectors in the 1980s. This was when the Class 20 fleet was allocated primarily to the Railfreight sector. The liberal application of Great Western chocolate brown paint is echoed by the golden ochre of the autumnal trees and hedges. Long shadows help highlight the passing train, much to the delight of railway photographers catching the last rays of sunshine, maybe until the winter steam trains carrying mince pies and Santa make their appearance.

Opposite below and right: Kingford, Wednesday 4 November 2020: Class 158 158798 passes with the 12.35 Barnstaple to Exeter St James Park and Class 158 158749 passes with the 13.35 Barnstaple to Exeter St James Park.

After their belated introduction to the Barnstaple branch, caused by the delay in Thames Chiltern releasing its turbo units to Bristol, these trains, either formed of two cars or three cars with an additional single Class 158 driving motor coach, provide a substantial improvement both in quality of ride and interior comfort when compared to the 'Pacer' and 'Sprinter' Class 150s that have dominated services on the Barnstaple branch over the last decade. At a journey length of one hour to traverse the full branch, this is certainly overdue. Atlantic Coast Express trains passing along the line destined for Ilfracombe would have provided a superior level of comfort for their passengers, but that would be an unfair comparison when referring to standard branch line stopping service trains. The line offers scenic vistas right from the start as it crosses the River Exe and then clambers up the valleys of the Rivers Yeo and Taw. Kingford is situated on the River Taw and is particularly colourful in the spring and autumn thanks to the many trees lining the valley.

Abbots Farm, Wednesday 4 November: Class 158 158951 passes with 14.11 St James Park to Barnstaple.
   The Barnstaple branch brushes past numerous farms and mills, reflecting both its agrarian and riverside territory. There are many bridges crossing the River Taw between Kings Nympton and Barnstaple as a result of the meandering nature of the river which the line closely follows for its route north of Eggesford. These all afford marvellous views along and over the river – photographers awaiting their next picture of a train crossing the river are quite likely to see either a kingfisher or a bird of prey – a hawk or an owl – seeking its next meal. The road that follows alongside is usually out of sight, and it is quite possible to consider yourself in the deepest of rural Devon while traversing the scenic landscape vistas that unfold in this section of the line.

Calstock Viaduct, Saturday 6 November 2010: View from the south-east.

This graceful and resplendent gem of engineering finesse at 120ft (36m) in height stretches over twelve 60ft (18m) wide arches along its 850ft (260m) length. Stepped corbels between each pair of arches form refuges in the parapet. The three central piers are on full display at low tide as they stand sentry-like above the river. At high tide, the minimum clearance for shipping is 110ft (34m). It traverses the border between Devon and Cornwall and in so doing adds an extra element of intrigue, for its grandiose composure belies the fact that it is not Great Western rails that it carries, but those of the intrepid LSWR-linked interloper. Its construction was completed in 1908, and it opened on 2 March, as part of the Plymouth, Devonport and South Western Junction Railway which had bought the East Cornwall Mineral Railway in 1894. The PD&SWJR was absorbed into the LSWR in 1923 when it was incorporated into the Southern Railway, and the line was worked by the LSWR.

To add insult to injury (on behalf of its promoters) the only other ways to reach Calstock by road from Devon was either by a lengthy detour via Tavistock or via the ferry from Saltash Passage on the Plymouth side of the River Tamar, passing virtually below the equally magnificent Royal Albert Bridge and crossing the Tamar at a wider point. The Callington branch was essentially a quiet rural line with agricultural produce and quarried stone as important as passengers. There were goods sidings and facilities at each of the stations on the branch, and there's the point – for the Tamar Valley's rich soils and gentle climate were (and are) ideal for growing vegetables and fruit, which the LSWR could then transport up to its larger customer base in London and those Home Counties which it served.

Opposite: Calstock Viaduct and Calstock Lower Kelly, Saturday 6 November 2010: View up-river from the north-west.

Here we see Calstock Viaduct as it crosses the River Tamar, with on the left near the boatyard the remains of a lime kiln at Lower Kelly. The tidal rise can be over 10ft (3m) at this point. The kiln was built in the early nineteenth century and raised in height around 1860, when the incline plane was constructed over the limekiln. The East Cornwall Mineral Railway rope-worked incline which descended to Calstock quay was about 800ft (244m) long and dropped down 350ft (106m) to reach the riverside quays. A stationary steam engine lowered the wagons down the 1 in 6 gradient over the last half-mile towards the quayside for eventual loading onto barges and schooners. Additionally there was a wagon lift which connected the quayside sidings to the line over the viaduct. This lift, built at the side of the viaduct, lowered single wagons to further sidings on the quay, 112ft (34m) below, and was served by sidings at Calstock station.

Below: Near Hood Bridge, South Devon Railway, Saturday 7 November 2009: Class 25 D7612 25262 hauls the 12.15 Buckfastleigh to Totnes.

The tranquil River Dart is closely followed by this preserved line in several parts of its journey to its ultimate destination of the sea at Dartmouth. It can, however, be a torrent after very heavy rain as the water descends from the rain-lashed moors at the back of Buckfastleigh and swells the river. Occasionally, the more courageous among local canoeists will venture out to ride the waters when this happens. It is interesting to note that several of the longer UK preserved railways follow river valleys, such as the Llangollen, Severn Valley and Churnet Valley railways, which is entirely understandable as the railway constructors sought to avoid gruelling gradients ascending hills and consequently their terrain was influenced by the routes that nature has carved out. Brunel's 'Atmospheric Railway', had it succeeded, would have seen trains far less deterred by gravity's limitations on speed, but thereby hangs another tale!

Above: Bethany, Thursday 19 November 2020: Great Western 'Castle' HST set passes with the 12.50 Penzance to Exeter St Davids.

The concept of the short four-car HST set has proved particularly successful in enabling the enhancement of services in Cornwall to and from Exeter, with some forming through services to Cardiff, and further previous mainline HST sets are undergoing conversion to short-formed versions for supplementing the fleet of these trains – all of which, alongside their regular scheduled maintenance, is certainly keeping Laira depot busy. They embrace the rolling Cornish landscape as if old partners, which of course they were in their traditional role of providing the mainstay of services to London Paddington until their withdrawal in May 2019. Compared to the previously provided alternative of a Class 150 'Sprinters' combined with a single Class 153, the quality of comfort and train performance is very significantly improved .

Opposite above: Bethany, Thursday 19 November 2020: Great Western 'Castle' HST set with power car 43154 *Compton Castle* passes with the 15.01 Plymouth to Penzance.

It's good to see the 'Castle' HST sets being named after various castles in the South West and Wales. This echoes their link with the Great Western 'Castle' 4073 class, with many of the 'Castle' HST sets so named sharing their identity with one of the former 4-6-0 steam locomotives, which when introduced were heralded as Britain's most powerful express passenger locomotive. The concept of giving locomotives a regional identity not only bonds them with the territory through which they pass but also links them with the key fortifications of the region's history - from vast fortresses overlooking the coast to former strategic strongholds, and others which remain inhabited to this day, strong and sturdy and often surrounded by myths and legends. They are testament to the engineering prowess of previous generations. In the same way, so also were the 'Castle' class steam locomotives and it may be that this accolade can now be appropriately awarded to these HST power cars which continue to give impressive service, for their design is truly a part of our heritage, having been first introduced to services to Devon and Cornwall in 1979.

Below: Bethany, Thursday 19 November 2020: Colas Class 70 70807 returns from Moorswater to Aberthaw with the last full-length cement train.

Bringing some welcome colour which corresponds well with the autumnal hues of the landscape's grasses and trees, and striding out past lengthening shadows, the Colas locomotive towing its heavy load would soon be history. For commercial reasons Tarmac had decided to close the Moorswater cement distribution depot and offices in mid-December and consequently this flow of freight into Cornwall came to an end. The old maxim of 'photograph what is ordinary today for it is tomorrow's history' rings all too true, although it is more pertinent when there are so very few freight trains along this stretch of track. Less to disturb the residents of the nearby farms – but will they really notice? Perhaps, for the throaty roar of the Class 70 can be heard well before it appears on the scene.

Liverpool Lime St, Friday 22 November 2019: Left, Northern Trains Class 331 331103 with a mid-morning service to Blackpool North; right, TransPennine Class 397 'Civity' in a special press promotional event.

The introduction of many new trains of different designs to large parts of the UK network in the 2019–2021 period has been astonishing and implemented at a swift pace. This event at Liverpool typifies the 'all change' nature of new arrivals complementing historic architectural contexts. Northern's three-car Class 331s made their service debut on 9 September 2019 with three diagrams being operated between Liverpool and Blackpool by these smart and comfortable units which commendably provide more tables alongside windows. The Class 397 TransPennine five-car EMUs are part of the CAF 'Civity' family of trains which will replace the ten four-car Class 350 Desiro units operating services between Liverpool, Manchester and Scotland. With a spacious and light interior, these also provide an improved level of comfort and quality. Alongside the new Class 68 hauled trains formed of TransPennine Mk 5 coaching stock to Scarborough, this dramatically revolutionises the train services emanating from Liverpool Lime Street. Such investment is overdue but impressive in its resulting display of new and impressive train fleets that surely must raise the profile of travel by train.

Kirkham and Wesham, Friday 22 November 2019: Northern Trains Class 195 passes with a driver training shuttle between Preston and Blackpool North, early afternoon.

    Another new train appearing in the North West is this Class 195 providing suburban and interregional services such as a newly introduced service from Chester to Leeds via Todmorden. The West Lancashire rich alluvial soil is well turned by the local horses here in the Fylde's typically flat countryside. The newly installed overhead wires indicate further investment which has, after many years of missed opportunities, finally seen electrification of the Blackpool North branch. This allows through workings by Pendolino electric units to London Euston without a requirement to change at Preston. It's a long time since Blackpool was so popular that summer Saturdays would see coaching stock from steam-hauled excursions and summer Saturday expresses stacked in all available sidings between Blackpool and many locations to the south along the West Coast Main Line. However it remains a popular year-round resort and draws on the conurbations of West Yorkshire, Greater Manchester and Merseyside (benefitting from new direct electric services as typified by the Class 331 in the photograph on page 172). The route's semaphore signalling and classic signal boxes have had to make way for this progress but it promises many improvements in travel to this part of Lancashire.

Laira Embankment, Wednesday 25 November 2020: Colas Class 70 70810 passes by the River Plym Estuary mid-morning with the final 6C35 Aberthaw to Moorswater (via Lostwithiel) cement train.

Late autumnal tints on the nearby moor and trees reflect the mood set by this train in its own late autumn, for it would regrettably no longer be seen passing the tranquil waters of the Plym Estuary on its weekly morning run to Moorswater. It had proved a focus for local photographers endeavouring to catch it on camera during its last few weeks, and was always interesting both as one of the few regular freight trains in the South West and as one hauled by one of the distinctive Colas liveried Class 70 locomotives. Railways do have their seasons as such, and they reflect such previous eras as those of steam and diesel locomotives hauling carriages past semaphore signals and signal boxes that have featured in past times as shown in this book. Yet in a few limited locations on the UK rail network it is still possible to breathe in the atmosphere of trains such as these when charter and excursion specials reactivate cherished memories of seasons past.

Polbathic Bridge, Near St Germans, Sunday 6 December 2020: Colas Class 66/8 66849 labours upgrade with the 10.10 Westbury to Penzance Long Rock civil engineers ballast train.

Long shadows of a late autumn early afternoon reach out towards the passing guest and the cool clear air reveals the extent of West Dartmoor in the background. Within a fortnight, the shortest day will restrict daytime photography to its least available time although the winter season has yet to announce its presence, apart from the autumnal frosts which hint at the occasional icy blast that will, apart from in milder winters, bestow Dartmoor with a mantle of snow which will thence cover the tapestry of autumnal colours with a blanket of purest white. Nature must hold its breath to find out if this part of east Cornwall will escape the rigours of the forthcoming winter, but for now it can bask in the final rays of gently warming sunshine.

Chapter 4
WINTER

Above and opposite above: Copplestone, 18 December 2010: First Great Western 'Pacer' Class 143 143619 at platform, then departing the snowbound station with the 11.27 Exeter St Davids to Barnstaple.

Note the differential speed signs here. The bottom one applies only to multiple units and shows 55mph is permissible whereas for any other class of rolling stock the top one showing 30mph applies. For example, a Class 66 or HST would be limited to 30mph. Many of the stations along the Barnstaple branch retain their original station buildings, a feature which contributes significantly to the character of the line with its many three-arch bridges crossing, especially but not exclusively, the southern half of the line where the Okehampton line ran parallel before it branched off. The platform may well have been cleared of snow after the first snowfall during this Arctic spell of weather but, left untouched, the depth of snow actually allows better grip for shoes and boots than a platform salted and yet still iced over in extreme weather such as this.

Below: Near Copplestone, Saturday 18 December 2010: First Great Western Class 150 passes with 11.43 Barnstaple, 12.20 to Exeter St Davids.

The snow-laden barren trees enshroud the passing train which leaves a trail of icy spray as it traverses a thoroughly white Devon landscape. In the south-west, it is usually later in January or February that snow makes an appearance, often restricted to the higher ground of Dartmoor and Exmoor, so this is quite early in the winter for there to be such a heavy pasting at lower levels. Assuming people are travelling to Exeter city on this final Saturday before Christmas in order to complete their Christmas shopping, they may wish to return early before the very cold evening sets in. They may need to purchase some skis if leaving their return train at some of the remote village halts!

Calstock, Sunday 20 December 2009: First Great Western Class 153 153318 descends the gradient with the 12.45 Gunnislake to Plymouth.

In this view taken overlooking the Tamar Valley from near Bere Alston on the Devon side of the river can be seen two of the typical signatures of farming land use in this region – sheep husbandry and vegetable cultivation in greenhouses. The fertile soils of the Tamar Valley and rich green grass lend themselves to this agricultural landscape in which can also can be found hops and plenty of fruit, for the milder winters here favour their bountiful growth. Many stables support the horse riders who meander around the quieter lanes with their steeds in this part of east Cornwall. Residents of the houses overlooking the river valley, along with passengers on board the train, will from here have a grandstand view of Calstock Viaduct as featured in several photographs elsewhere in this book.

Blachford Viaduct, Tuesday 21 December 2010: First Great Western HST power car 43097 *Environment Agency* at rear of the late-running 09.06 London Paddington to Plymouth.

    Passengers are rewarded with this view towards Dartmoor with, on the left, Penn Moor (1,617ft, 493m) and Stall Moor (1,303ft, 397m) to the right. The blue livery was better for photography in conditions such as this whereas the Great Western green later applied to the HST fleet tended to struggle to be noticed. The barren tree reinforces the fact that all the leaves have fallen and the winter season has truly arrived in style. The clear cold air helps to provide unimpeded visibility which reveals the details of fields and woods on the lower slopes of this western side of Dartmoor.

Above left: Blachford Viaduct, Tuesday 21 December 2010: CrossCountry Class 221 'Super Voyager' forms the late running 09.12 Birmingham New Street (06.32 ex-York) to Plymouth.

Although the cramped and plastic interiors of these units leaves much to be desired, even endured by those who are travelling long distances, their exterior train design has a certain attractive appeal which is sometimes overlooked in the mundane but relatively reliable duties they fulfil. No doubt a very busy train earlier in its journey through the populous South Yorkshire and West Midlands, with passengers travelling home or to visit family for the forthcoming Christmas break, it will soon reach its destination and hence be ready for its return journey with less layover time than is built in for such recovery.

Above right: Blachford Viaduct, Tuesday 21 December 2010: First Great Western HST forming 12.55 Plymouth to London Paddington, with power car 43097 *Environment Agency* making a second appearance for the photographer.

The reliability of these HSTs with their high degree of comfort and sturdy ride sustained them in service on the Great Western main line for just under a further ten years after this photograph was taken. With a full breakfast available on the early morning service to businessmen and women travelling to important meetings in the capital, and a dinner available on the return, they were very much preferred to the option of flying – a choice removed in early 2011 when flights from Plymouth were withdrawn. They swallowed up with ease the huge crowds of holiday makers heading for the south-west in summer, with ample space for surfboards on services extending to Newquay. They became established as a flagship of long-distance quality, with a frequently offered chance to upgrade during the journey to first class subject to availability – an appealing option with unlimited coffee or tea and biscuits for those lucky enough to take up the offer. The author cannot say anything quite so praiseworthy about their replacements, the Class 800 IETs, although they are earning their own way towards stardom but with less panache.

Buckfastleigh, South Devon Railway, Tuesday 21 December 2010: GWR Class 2884 2-8-0 3803 arrives on 14.15 'Santa Special' from Totnes.

'Santa Specials' have a triple appeal. They provide a genuine treat for the very youngest passengers to experience meeting Father Christmas and receiving a special toy. They may not be too worried about being hauled by a steam engine at the same time although they certainly enjoy the whistles and hiss of steam emanating from the green giant at the front. It's a special celebration of the Christmas season for parents wishing to fill each day of Christmas with something memorable and worthwhile. For the preserved railway, it can prove one of the most financially beneficial events of the year. Volunteers are usually available during the holiday to carry the trays of mince pies and orange juice or punch to the happy passengers and everyone works as a team to ensure that the customers have a thoroughly enjoyable experience. Additionally, for photographers there is an extra opportunity to catch steam in action before the lull in timetabled trains during the early months of the new year. With a welcome fall of snow to enhance the atmosphere and low sunshine to bestow the hoped-for glint off the locomotive, it combines a perfect scene with a contented trainload of delighted travellers.

Exeter St Davids, Saturday 18 December 2010: South West Trains Class 159 159005 departs with 11.26 to Axminster – the line beyond, towards Salisbury, was closed due to 'adverse railhead conditions'.

The modern railway is less easy to capture in scenes incorporating snow and shadows such as this, for there is no billowing steam or expression of movement in the same way as in scenes in which a steam locomotive features. However, the faint exhaust and silhouette still permit some idea of the chill and impression of a solitary diesel unit emerging from the sanctuary of the station to engage with the wintry conditions which lie ahead on its journey, on this occasion curtailed at Axminster. It's a very peaceful scene – any hustle and bustle for the Christmas shopping on this last Saturday before Christmas Day is more likely to occur at Exeter Central, which is at the top of the ascent faced by this train, for it is located closer to the city centre.

Exeter St Davids, Friday 24 December 2010: First Great Western Class 142 142063 in North Western Trains livery, departs with the 10.56 to Paignton.

It is unlikely that many travellers on this service to Paignton will be heading for the beach, or even a swim, but the larger Torbay hotels will be busy with guests arriving on this Christmas Eve for their special Christmas stay, and the chefs will be busy preparing the ingredients for the luxurious Christmas meals that their guests will be excitedly anticipating. There will be no trains running over the next couple of days but vast civil engineering projects will take advantage of the national lull and engineers will work to tight deadlines at many locations across the country. They are an unseen workforce who give up their Christmas as part of this grandiose effort to improve the network without being interrupted by the daily flow of trains. They indeed deserve a glass raising with applause for such magnanimous commitment.

Exeter St Davids, Friday 24 December 2010: First Great Western HST power car 43094 leads the arriving 09.06 London Paddington to Plymouth.

In steam days, it was possible for a journey to Plymouth to depart from either the north or south end of this station. Trains to Plymouth via Okehampton and Tavistock would depart in a northerly direction, branching off the up main on their circuitous route at Cowley Bridge Junction while trains for Plymouth and Penzance via Newton Abbot departed towards the south. Now, up departures for London Waterloo depart from the down Platform 1 at Exeter but branch off immediately after departure on the section of line to Exeter Central's up platform. A Class 159 can be seen awaiting such a turn in the down sidings to the right of the arriving HST. It is such quirks of railway history that provide additional interest and intrigue to Britain's network of lines.

Yeoford, Friday 24 December 2010: First Great Western Class 153 153361 departs with the 11.27 Exeter St Davids to Barnstaple.

This makes an interesting contrast with the autumnal scene in Yeoford on Saturday 30 October 2010, featured on page 160. The Okehampton branch rails and sleepers are entirely encased in snow. The snow-covered bush ascending from the disused down platform disguises where there were once steps leading up to the road bridge on this east side of the bridge parapet. This is an unusually heavy snowfall for this part of the UK, and the author crossed the frozen River Yeo on his walk through the spectacular white landscape surrounding Yeoford. The Arctic air is crystal clear and the deep blue of the sky a rare event in December, when leaden skies, south-westerly gales and rain are the usual weather to endure.

Yeoford, Friday 24 December 2010: First Great Western Class 142 142064 in North Western Trains livery arrives with the 11.43 Barnstaple to Exmouth.

On the left, clearly unused at this point as indicated by the undisturbed snow on the rails, is the Okehampton branch, which actually *was* being used at this time from Okehampton to just as far as where Coleford Junction was situated (where the line diverged a little over a mile or so away from here). The occasion for this was the annual 'Polar Express' special trains which were making their festive appearance for the Christmas season, and indeed early in the new year an opportunity to travel the line between the two Class 31 locomotives used to haul the 'Polar Express' stock was offered for local rail enthusiasts, as seen in the photographs of Class 31/4 31454 at Okehampton and Sampford Courtenay on page 192.

British American Railway Services (BARS) put the Okehampton line up for sale in 2019, having reopened it in 2009. The company's subsequent fortunes were somewhat diminished two years later when Meldon Quarry, which had continued to be accessed by rail, closed. This was because Bardon Aggregates, the quarry's owner, withdrew granite production at Meldon after a reduction in the demand for rail ballast. There were plans to restore and reopen the down platform at Yeoford station and to operate an open access service from Okehampton to Exeter, but this was never realised and indeed the latter took place in November 2021, although even then this station remained bypassed by the restored Okehampton services. The Dartmoor Railway Supporters' Association consequently provided rolling stock, staff and volunteers for the line's operation in quasi-preservation, including the seasonal heritage services at the Dartmoor Railway, and Okehampton station was carefully maintained with a number of facilities. The reopening of the Okehampton branch, therefore sees a very significant step in the survival of the line which, after the quarry closed, was living on borrowed time.

Yeoford, Friday 24 December 2010: First Great Western Class 142 142064 in North Western Trains livery departs with 11.43 Barnstaple to Exmouth.

Most of this class of 'Pacer' diesel unit had been withdrawn across the country, where used, by December 2019 with a handful retained by Northern (which had the majority in service) for a couple of months afterwards and several units kept in reserve. Interestingly 142001 has been preserved as an example of these railcars for the National Collection, and it is planned for it to provide rides both at the NRM and the Science Museum's various other sites. Several preserved railways have purchased withdrawn 'Pacers' – at give-away prices – where their use is seen valuable for off peak and 'quiet' times of day. The island platform once housed a refreshments room catering for the needs of passengers transferring between the North Devon line and the line to Okehampton, Tavistock and Plymouth.

Neopardy Cottages, Friday 24 December 2010: First Great Western Class 142 142029 in North Western Trains livery approaches with the 12.53 Exmouth to Barnstaple.

Note here the Okehampton branch rails and sleepers encased in snow, and also the characteristic lineside hut, which is unusually built of wood rather than being one of many of the Southern Railway concrete type found on this line and also featuring frequently on the Exeter to Waterloo line. The pink hue of the clouds promises a sunset and a further fine and sunny Christmas Day ahead. The long-reaching shadows so early in the afternoon remind us how short the daylight is at this time, close to the winter solstice. In the northern hemisphere, astronomers and scientists use the December solstice as the start of the winter season, which ends on the March equinox. For meteorologists, on the other hand, winter began three weeks before on 1 December. The December solstice occurs when the sun reaches its most southerly declination of -23.4 degrees. In other words, when the North Pole is tilted furthest away from the sun. The December solstice can happen on December 20, 21, 22 or 23, although the shortest day is formally observed as Monday 21 December.

Crowcombe, West Somerset Railway, Sunday 28 December 2008: GWR 0-6-2T 5600 Class 6695 hauling the 10.30 Minehead to Bishops Lydeard.

The morning frost retains its icy grip into the early afternoon here, where the low sunlight has just arrived. Meanwhile the Quantocks enjoy the limited warmth offered on this perfect winter's day. Photographer's can enjoy the benefits provided by its lucky coincidence with the railway's winter steam gala. Assured of bountiful quantities of steam which occasionally threaten to enshroud the locomotive at times, especially during its recent clamber up the demanding gradient all the way from Williton, the cool air mingles with the shadows from the trees to provide a memorable recollection of a Great Western branch line passenger train wending its way through the west Somerset countryside.

Crowcombe, West Somerset Railway, Thursday 29 December 2005: GWR Class 4500 2-6-2T 5553 awaits departure with the 15.45 Bishops Lydeard to Minehead.

  No wonder the general public, rail enthusiasts and photographers welcome snow when it is combined with steam. The scene exudes atmosphere with the fading light of dusk relieved by the warm glow emanating from the traditional platform lamps and tungsten yellow light from the signal box. Steam heating escapes between the carriages and the festive Christmas star and decorations are almost hiding by the waiting room. This locomotive was visiting from the Swanage Railway.

Allerton, Saturday 30 December 2000: Virgin Class 86/2 86256 *Pebble Mill* hauls a predominantly InterCity liveried set of ECS to Allerton carriage sidings.

This station has since received a substantial rebuild to accommodate interchange between the Merseyrail Northern lines and the main line to the south along with the Cheshire Lines Railway route to Manchester. It has been renamed Liverpool South Parkway, and bus connections to Liverpool John Lennon Airport are also available from the forecourt. For passengers from the north of Liverpool travelling via Liverpool Central to Manchester Piccadilly or Sheffield, it avoids any necessity for a short-distance walk between Liverpool Central and Liverpool Lime Street stations, which adds time and inconvenience. The Class 86s looked colourful in the Virgin Trains livery, even if such workings as shown here were an everyday feature of the railway landscape.

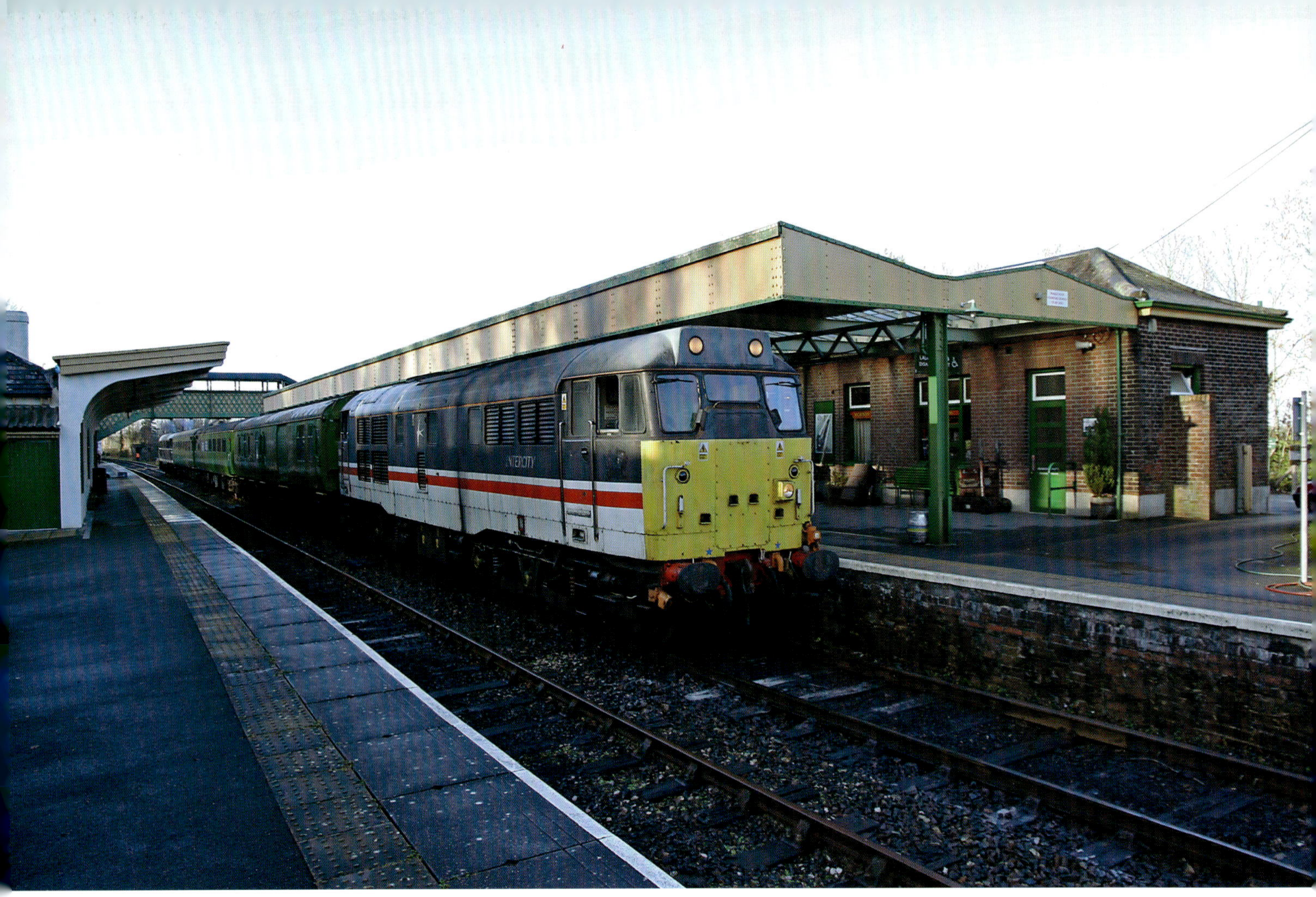
INTERCITY

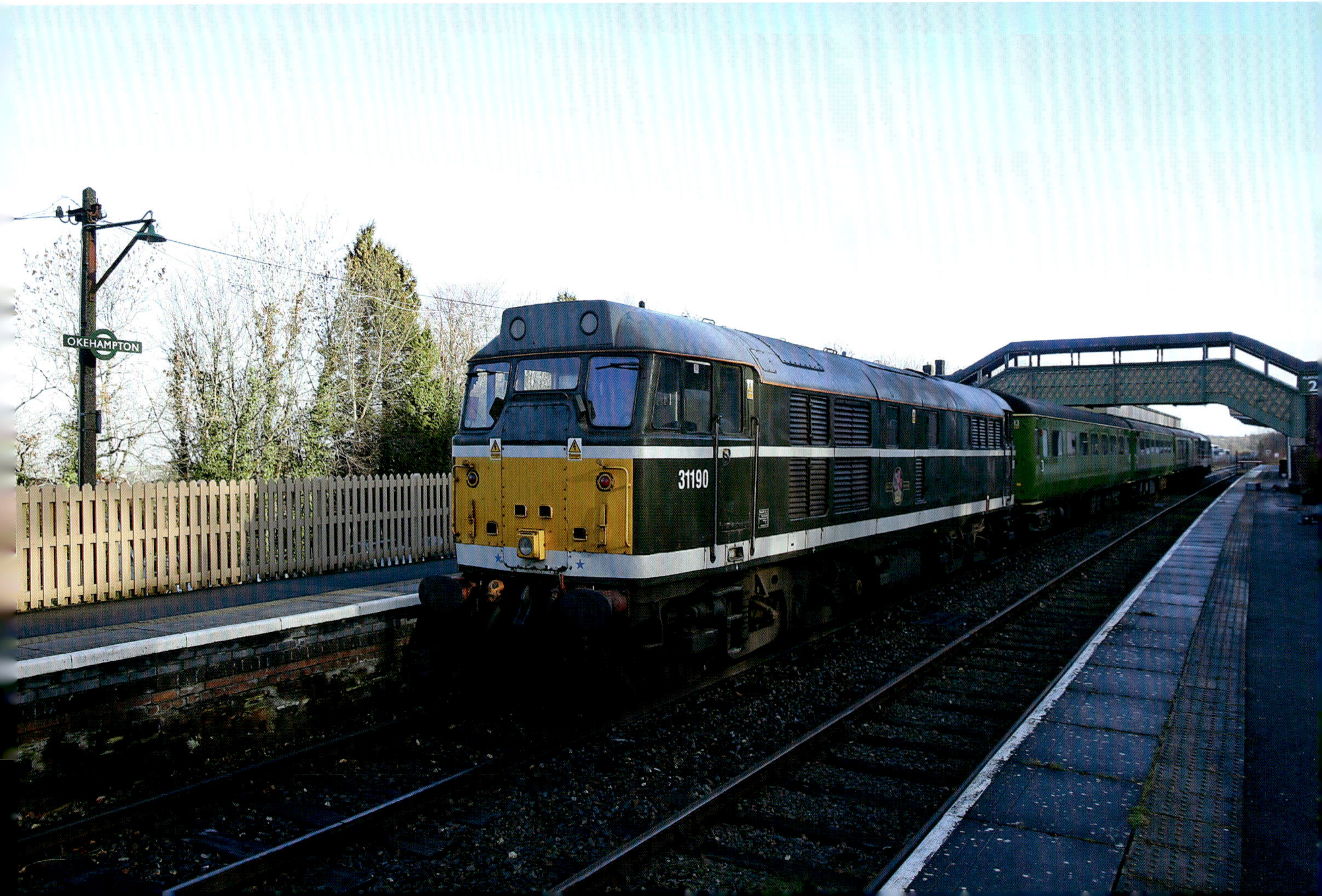
OKEHAMPTON
31190
2

Opposite: Okehampton, Dartmoor Railway Sunday 9 January 2011: Class 31/4 31454 in InterCity livery arrives with the 12.05 for Coleford Junction, formed of coaching stock including Pressed Steel Class 117 59520 (preserved by the Dartmoor Railway) and Class 31 31190 in BR green livery at rear, both owned by BARS.

This was an event organised before both locomotives returned north after their use with the very popular and remunerative 'Polar Express' trains over the Christmas period. Okehampton station retains its Southern Railway features including the canopy and footbridge – all touched up in relevant Southern green paintwork – accompanied by a few items of platform furniture and station signposts which further help to capture the past. It all looks well kept for an otherwise disused station, at least until the timetabled summer Sunday trains return, although it will have been spruced up for the 'Polar Express' clientele. The station's late closure date in 1972 along with the line's continued use thereafter by quarried stone trains from nearby Meldon Quarry meant that fortunately the buildings were not demolished with the haste that some lines closed in the Beeching era experienced.

Class 31 31454, when one of the Fragonset Class 31s used in top and tail mode on the Bristol to Weymouth and Cardiff to Brighton services operated by Wessex Trains in 2004, received its InterCity livery to match that carried by the coaches formed in the stock provided for this service (which was not just during the summer timetable). Later in that decade it would be seen providing traction for Network Rail test trains.

Below: Sampford Courtenay, Dartmoor Railway, Sunday 9 January 2011: Class 31 31190, in BR green livery, at rear and Class 31/4 31454, in InterCity livery leading with the 12.05 Okehampton to Coleford Junction.

'Next stop Wadebridge then Padstow?' It could be – at an incredibly long stretch of the imagination, although the fact that the route has been relaid for daily service does not make it likely we will be seeing the likes of these two vintage diesels in charge of such services. Alas we must be resigned to the fact that much of the 'Withered Arm' route beyond Okehampton is most unlikely to see rails re-laid apart from a very distant possibility of the Tavistock to Okehampton section being reinstated. The rolling Devon countryside in the distance to the north of Yeoford draws the eye away from the surprisingly gold tinted trees encroaching on the line just west of Sampford Courtenay. These will need significant lopping before the planned weekday passenger service is introduced, especially if it occurs during autumn's leaf fall – otherwise passengers will be better bringing their sledges, for the rail surfaces will be submerged by leaf mulch. Considering it's all downhill to Coleford, 31190 seems to be emitting a lot of exhaust, which will not keep the local environmentalists happy, but perhaps the newly reinstated train service will relieve the congested roads into Exeter which will help alleviate their concerns.

Stoke, Plymouth, Saturday 19 January 1985: Class 47/4 47618 on a mid-morning eastbound InterCity service.

  It is interesting to reflect on the fact that the Class 47 locomotives proved so versatile they could be entrusted to moving most types of railway traffic with generally proven reliability. Perhaps they were somewhat disregarded by photographers because they were so numerous and could be seen countrywide, and because smaller classes of locomotive tended to have a more interesting 'perceived 'character. If there was only a small batch that had been produced, their appeal would maybe have matched that given to Class 31 or 45 locomotives. Even in preservation, they tend to need a livery other than BR blue to add interest to their appearance within the camera frame. Passengers on board this service can be assured of plenty of electric train heat keeping them comfortably warm. The snowfall is unusually heavy for the South West.

Laira Embankment, Tuesday 21 January 2020: Great Western paired Class 801 units depart with the 09.15 Plymouth to London Paddington.

It's a heavy frost on the main line and on those rails feeding into Laira depot behind the photographer. The early morning mist is slowly dissipating and the tide will soon return to cover the mud and seaweed of the estuary. The gentle if subdued sunlight helps to draw out the surrounding colours in a less vivid manner than that seen during the summer, and it almost seems more natural in this midwinter scene. The snakelike intercity express train (IET) passes through with no sense of rushing, appearing as if a guest invited, though all too briefly for it must soon tackle the gradient up Hemerdon which will require some applied exertion and effort to keep up the pace required by the scheduled diagram.

Laira Embankment, Tuesday 21 January 2020: CrossCountry Class 221 'Super Voyager' passes along the Plym embankment with the 09.27 Plymouth to Aberdeen.

   Gleaming in the early morning rays of sunshine, and caught passing nearby to the peaceful reflections from the estuary, this train's participation in an otherwise everyday scene acquires the qualities that reward a landscape painter's special portrayal of this winter's day. The cool, clear air and sublime sunlight combine to enhance the panorama at just the right time for capturing the passing train on which some passengers may be travelling almost the length of the country. The light will soon change, the mist will have evaporated and the tide will start to lap the channels bereft of seawater. Then an entirely different vista will slowly emerge. The camera merely captures the essence of the moment and provides a reminder of this wonderful spectacle.

Plymouth Station, Saturday 31 January 1987: At right is Class 50 50007 *Conqueror* with Mk 1 ECS; centre is Scottish Class 47/4 47551 (based at Eastfield) on a Plymouth Argyle FC supporters special to Arsenal.

This shows an interesting assemblage of British Railways traction typical of the mid-1980s, but less typical to Plymouth was this Scottish Class 47/4 and also Scottish Class 47/4 47469 *Glasgow Chamber of Commerce* (very recently transferred to Inverness from Eastfield) and another Scottish Class 47 which had left preceding this scene with further Plymouth Argyle FC supporter trains. Clearly there was extra coaching stock available to meet this type of surge in demand – a far cry from the twenty-first-century railway where stock shortages require substitute locomotive-hauled stock, or even 'bustitution' in certain areas of the country. Some enthusiasts used to travel on the special football supporters' trains provided in order to achieve 'haulage' behind locomotives unusually featuring on passenger stock. The Class 08 locomotives continued to find employment well into the second decade of the twenty-first century, but the parcels and mail traffic such as attached to the Class 08 in the bay platform are regrettably a long distant memory.

Tavistock Junction, Friday 1 February 1991: Class 47/4 47801 passes with the 12.15 Plymouth to Manchester Piccadilly.

The combined BR blue livery of the locomotive and InterCity livery of the coaches (with the exception of the buffet vehicle) blend well together and reinforce the business-like approach to travel that was increasingly part of the 1990s' scene. This is echoed by the Railfreight 'Speedlink' vans stabled on the right. Speedlink was a brand name given to a traditional freight distribution service established in 1983 involving individual wagons which originated from various separate road distribution centres (both railway and privately owned) and individual factory sidings which were shunted into a single train at the nearest Speedlink regional centre. Upon arrival at the appropriate regional centre for distribution, wagons would then be sorted and delivered to their separate destinations. This service was faster than existing freights, had a higher haulage capacity and avoided the need for large marshalling yards. Speedlink remained part of the Railfreight division, but with its own distinguishing red, yellow and grey livery as seen on this set of wagons.

Stoke, Plymouth, Saturday 8 February 1986: A Class 50 passes with the 07.50 Bristol to Penzance.

In the 1980s you could enjoy locomotive-hauled travel across most parts of the BR network, except in the south-east which was dominated by the ubiquitous EMUs. This regional service would become a single Class 150 'Sprinter' diesel unit (possibly with a Class 153 attached if strengthening was perceived necessary) during later years – hardly appropriate for a journey lasting potentially three and a half hours – although, fortunately, this has now been replaced by 'Castle' class short HST sets with smartly refurbished interiors following their withdrawal from London services and reassignment to services between Cardiff and Penzance.

Laira Depot, Sunday 10 February 1991: from left to right, nearest is Class 37/6 37674 with Railfreight Distribution decals, and Class 47/4 47628 in InterCity livery. Centre far left is a Network SouthEast livery Class 50, adjacent to a Class 50 in BR large logo blue livery, then Class 50 50008 *Thunderer* in full BR blue livery, and at the right of the line-up is Class 50 50015 *Valiant* in civil engineers grey and yellow livery. Class 101 Metro-Cammell and Class 108 DMUs feature on the right.

How interesting our diesel depots were, providing a feast of locomotives on shed at weekends. The variety of types of locomotive and liveries kept photographers bemused then, when trying to capture each variant on camera, and also now when, like your author, they pore over the details and reminisce about the locomotives which featured in those same photographs. Even the DMUs provide some interest in their own liveries and designs. Of course, subtle changes in types of locomotive would occur over the post-steam decades, each demonstrating the changing demands from fleet managers. Twenty years previous to this photograph would have seen the diesel hydraulic 'Westerns' and 'Warships', along with 'Peaks' and Class 47s – some still wearing green livery – dominating the scene. It is encouraging to know that Laira Traction & Rolling Stock Maintenance Depot has found an enhanced role in the new railway landscape that is in place now the Great Western HST fleet has been withdrawn. It remains busy managing rolling stock from Great Western and the CrossCountry HST fleets and in a wider context as an engineering and maintenance facility par excellence.

Beare Mill Farm and countryside to the north of Crediton, Saturday 12 February 2011: First Great Western 'Pacer' Class 143 leads First Great Western Class 153 single railcar with 12.53 Exmouth, 13.27 Exeter St Davids to Barnstaple.

This eye-catching photograph shows a train which has just passed Beare Mill farm which can be seen on the far right, close to Salmon Pool Crossing. The landscape's very character adds colour to the rich tapestry of fields with the Devon Redlands soils clearly evident where ploughed. The underlying red sandstone and consequent red soil dominate the landscape and are part of the red colour found in the traditional stone and cob farmsteads, hamlets and villages that are scattered across the area. This very fertile soil makes this the agricultural heart of Devon. The gently rolling hills reveal a network of hedgerows enclosing relatively small fields containing either sheep or cultivation of crops. The hedgerow trees and small copses often give a wooded appearance to the hills. This is a picturesque vista for every season!

Laira Depot, Monday 18 February 1991: Class 50s pass with, at front, 50017 *Royal Oak* and second, 50030 *Repulse* with eastbound Network SouthEast ECS for a mid-morning Exeter St Davids to London Waterloo service. In the foreground is seen Class 47/4 47802 in a light engine movement. Meanwhile a Class 08 undertakes a shunting movement with a BR Grampus ballast wagon (part of the departmental fleet) and an HST power car features on the right.

Here's a reminder that the Network SouthEast livery was introduced in June 1986, so its appearance on both of the locomotives and coaching stock was well established by the time of this photograph. It's a busy scene with a lot happening all at the same time. The HST power car cab looks new and may well have been fitted at Laira during a very recent visit to the works. The Class 08 enjoys showing off its newly applied Railfreight grey, no doubt applied by Laira's skilled apprentices.

No. 50017 *Royal Oak* worked its last train in September 1991 and was withdrawn the same month due to main generator damage. No. 50030 *Repulse* here carries the lighter shade of Network SouthEast scheme 2 blue livery. Grampus wagons were used to take spoil, so the Class 08 is probably shunting an engineering train in the siding. It carries BR olive green paintwork.

202 • BRITAIN'S RAILWAYS THROUGH THE SEASONS

Scorton, Friday 20 February 2004: EWS Class 66 66086 with midday northbound empty coal HAAs probably heading for Hunterston from Rugeley power station.

    This section of the West Coast Main Line is often overlooked in favour of its more northerly neighbours running through the dramatic scenery of the Lake District and Cumbrian mountains. The River Wyre which passes close by this location flows along the edge of and originates in the Bowland Fells. This is an area of gentle and tidy lowlands, criss-crossed with dry stone walls and dotted with picturesque farms and villages. Today sheep and beef farming predominates in the uplands with dairying being the major land use in the valleys. The extensive heather moorland has largely been conserved because of management for grouse shooting. It is designated an Area of Outstanding Natural Beauty.

    It is interesting to muse how over the decades the transport of coal by rail has changed. In steam days this train might have been formed of a lengthy trail of unfitted wagons hauled by an LMS 0-6-0 Class 4F assisted up the grades by a second locomotive at the rear, or later by a BR 2-10-0 Class 9F giving a solitary but equally impressive performance – each would have produced atmospheric and dramatic steam images to linger long in the memory after such trains had faded into history.

Scorton, Friday 20 February 2004: Class 92 passes with southbound ex-Royal Mail vans, now redundant, operated as a WCML route-learning train from Crewe South Yard to Carnforth return working.

When they were introduced in the mid-1990s, Class 92s were all fitted with three 'O' shaped tunnel logos to reflect their intended use on international freight trains and certain proposed passenger services to and through the Channel Tunnel, as seen on this locomotive. However the class has had a rather chequered history. Their high electrical power rating meant that Railtrack barred the type from its intended purpose of hauling traffic over the Wembley to Dollands Moor route via Redhill. Significant problems resulted from their inability to meet the new signalling interference criteria laid down by Railtrack, which led to the remarkable situation of the type being banned from operating over the section of line which gave access to its home depot at Crewe. As a result, these engines had to be dragged there from as far away as Wembley. Furthermore, the 'Nightstar' sleeper project which was to see their use on international trains to the Continent was repeatedly delayed owing to overrunning costs and difficulty in finding a contractor to build the carriages. Although assembly of the Nightstar stock began, 'London & Continental Railways' (the privatised company originally established in 1994 to own European Passenger Services International) decided to abandon the project because of escalating costs, all of which left seven of the class without any work.

Their use this century has been primarily with DB Cargo, which owns seventeen of the fleet, hauling container trains on the West Coast Main Line. GB Railfreight now owns sixteen, and as from April 2015 commenced a contract to supply the traction and drivers for the 'Caledonian Sleeper' trains from London Euston to Edinburgh and Glasgow. This required refreshment of some of their fleet which had been stored out of use for over a decade, and ten Class 92 locomotives were refurbished and modified for use with the new Mk 5 coaches. Several of the others ended up in Bulgaria under the banner of DB Cargo Bulgaria.

Scorton, Friday 20 February 2004: A pair of Class 175/0 'Coradia' two-car DMUs in First North Western livery operating the 12.15 Windermere to Manchester Airport , a First North Western service.

These express DMUs have proved popular with passengers thanks to their generous leg room and comfortable interiors. Originally built for service with First North Western, changes to franchises over time meant that although all were leased by Arriva Trains Wales, sub-leasing arrangements from February 2004 in turn meant that Chester depot, where they were all based, had to supply a daily allocation to three different train companies: Arriva Trains Wales, First North Western and Trans Pennine Express. Once the Class 185 units were newly introduced to Trans Pennine in 2006–07, this fleet became wholly dedicated to Arriva Trains Wales. All then received Arriva's turquoise blue and cream livery, and many now display the Transport for Wales livery – white with a broad red stripe at cantrail level, and red doors.

Catterall, Friday 20 February 2004: EWS Class 66 66170 with a southbound loaded coal train probably from Hunterston to Rugeley power station, passing a Class 175/1 'Coradia' three-car DMU in First North Western livery operating the 13.49 Manchester Airport to Barrow-in-Furness, a First North Western service.

  The low winter's afternoon light illuminates these two very different trains, which illustrate how busy the West Coast Main Line can be, north of Preston. The rapid loss of coal traffic to rail as biomass and gas-fired alternative fuels replaced it took many railway photographers by surprise, for such trains were an integral part of the railway landscape taken for granted, and their decline meant fewer types of traffic to capture on camera countrywide. All part of the increasing need to restrict CO_2 and greenhouse gas emissions resulting from the burning of fossil fuels for energy and cement production. At nearly 370 million tonnes annual total CO_2 emissions by the UK in 2019, it's a lot better than the 660.39 million tonnes in 1971's annual total. However, the damage has been done and there is a recognised global responsibility to swiftly reduce these emissions further. Fortunately, rail travel offers the chance to make a real impact either on a daily commute or longer distance business or leisure trips.

Stoke Cutting, Devonport, Saturday 10 March 2007: First Great Western Class 57 57605 *Totnes Castle* hauls sleeper coaches forming the 1A88 10.32 Penzance to Plymouth Laira as a result of engineering works closing the Cornish main line overnight which prevented this running in its normal diagram.

Scheduled sleeper trains are a rare event in the UK, mainly because most of the English cities are within a four- or five-hour drive of the capital. Where the distance and time involved is longer, then the viable option of providing a sleeper service becomes appealing, and the 'West Country Sleeper' is very popular with business and leisure travellers alike. Whereas the 'Caledonian Sleeper' uses state-of-the-art brand-new coaches which almost need a small power station to run all the demands required, the West Country Sleepers are less glitzy but still very comfortable, and there is seated accommodation for those not requiring a berth. It is interesting to note that even in mainland Europe, there was a sharp decline in the provision of sleeper services after 2012 – in part because TGVs slashed daytime travel times between northern and southern France, and also because the German railway services that ran under the 'City Night Line' brand within Germany, serving neighbouring European countries, were withdrawn in December 2016, having proved unprofitable. ÖBB (Austrian Railways) has subsequently relaunched a whole network of overnight sleeper services serving popular routes from Austria and Switzerland to northern Germany and also from Munich to Milan, Rome, Venice and Budapest under the 'NightJet' banner, offering sleeper, couchette or seated accommodation. This has proved a great success – and at prices suited to many rather than the more luxury end of the market that the Caledonian Sleeper seems to be aimed at.

Stoke Cutting, Devonport, 12 March 2021: LNER power car 43299 at the rear of the 06.08 Reading Triangle to Paignton via Penzance NMT seen heading into Plymouth en route to Paignton.

As we saw in an earlier photograph, there is a monthly visit by this train monitoring the rails along the main line to Penzance, and a newly acquired HST power car in the spring of 2021 added a further splash of colour to this visitor to the south-west. This had become available as a result of the influx of 'Azuma' IETs to services along the East Coast Main Line, and the consequent displacement of the HST fleet along these rails. The fact that these power cars are still proving useful in their 'extended' later lives is testimony to the success and durability of this design of train which was certainly revolutionary when first introduced to service and still provides sterling service for some CrossCountry services. Not so the case with some of their replacement Class 800/801/802 long-distance IETs operated by Great Western Railway, London North Eastern Railway, TransPennine Express and Hull Trains. These were completely withdrawn from service as a precaution on 8 May 2021 following the discovery of cracks in the jack points underneath the coaches of some of these trains. Fortunately a solution has been found and the problem was relatively temporary if very disruptive.

Richmond Bridge, Wednesday 11 March 2020: South Western Railway Class 707 passes with a mid-afternoon train bound for Windsor and Eton Riverside. Richmond bathes in late winter sunshine.

Nice livery, but unwanted! This new fleet of trains with spacious accommodation and a very smooth ride was intended for suburban services in the south-west of London. However, the thirty five-car Class 707 units will transfer over to SouthEastern when they are made redundant by South Western Railway. They will be replaced by ninety Class 701 'Aventra' trains, which are on order from Bombardier for South Western Railway, which will be used on 'Metro' services (such as illustrated here) from London Waterloo. This is all a result of a change of franchise, with a different type of train preferred by the new incumbent. This wouldn't happen in France where the rail service still exists in a quasi-nationalised state, but increasingly even there, the regions are starting to specify preferred types of train for their routes and making their voices heard a little louder, if so far overlooked by the movers and shakers in control.

Watchet, West Somerset Railway, Sunday 17 March 1991: Class 52 'Western' D1035 *Western Yeoman* (ex-*Western Campaigner*) passes with the 13.45 Minehead to Bishops Lydeard.

Not only did the Western Region prefer to differ from other regions in its choice of hydraulic transmission for the early fleet of diesels but 'Western' class locomotives also received a number of trial liveries in their careers. The first 'Western', D1000 *Western Enterprise*, was outshopped in a unique desert sand livery with wheels, roof panels, bogies and window frames in black. Being a rather light colour, it would have been harder to keep clean in the type of heavy service that these locomotives undertook. Within three years, it would wear the more traditional maroon livery applied to the rest of the fleet.

Early trade through the once busy Watchet harbour included the export of a superior lime produced from the numerous lime kilns along the coast. Alabaster and gypsum were also notable trades out of the port for use in the paper industry, ornaments and chimney manufacture. Fish and agricultural products, wool and hides were important exports, alongside cloth manufactured at the local mills. Salt, coal, wines and brandy were imports from the Continent. More recently, there were regular imports of timber from Russia and Scandinavia, and wine from Portugal and the Mediterranean. Some exports of car parts, tractors and other industrial goods (mainly from the Midlands) demonstrates how competitive Watchet was. Over time, the harbour was unable to compete and was decommissioned for commercial traffic in 1999.

Watchet, West Somerset Railway, Sunday 17 March 1991: Class 35 'Hymek' D7017 with the 13.50 Bishops Lydeard to Minehead, view towards Doniford Beach and the Quantock Hills.

    Could we say that for each livery carried, the locomotive traverses its own series of seasons? From spring BR green to summer BR blue; from spring BR green carried by the Westerns to autumnal BR maroon and then to summer BR blue. That's a strange sequence not mirrored in nature! Also, which colour is winter to be? I haven't seen many white locomotives although maybe the 'InterCity Swallow' livery of the 1990s could count as it was part-white? Furthermore, swallows are summer visitors to the UK. They start to arrive here from Africa in April, and return in September – a seasonal migration. Or could it be that each coat of colour is worn for an era before the next is applied – so from nationalised railway livery to private sector livery – and then what happens to Transport for Wales livery, which is a further digression? Which season is a NMT yellow HST? Or what about Porterbrook which painted some locomotives in its purple house colours? Yellow could represent summer sunshine or autumnal gold. Maybe we should simply say that no such parallel fully exists outside nature's ever rich tapestry throughout the seasons.

Castle Hill, West Somerset Railway, Saturday 19 March 2011: GWR Class 5101 2-6-2T 4160 climbs with the 10.00 Minehead to Bishops Lydeard.

   A reminder that with our following the astronomical seasons, spring starts on 20 March, yet clearly this scene could well be winter with the trees still awaiting any sign of warmth to spur their leaves into growth and the steam trail echoing the cool air of the chilled morning. However, the sun is much brighter than in the depths of winter and will bring a sense of cheer and promise of warmer days to come. The steam exhaust creates its slight shadow over the foremost carriages but all else is waking up to greet the fine blue skies and perfect conditions for this locomotive to demonstrate its power and prowess as it engages with the steady ascent that lies before it.

Lower Bye Farm, West Somerset Railway, Saturday 19 March 2011: BR Class 7MT 4-6-2 70000 *Britannia* storms up Washford Bank with the 12.00 Bishops Lydeard to Minehead.

The trees form an arch to welcome the passing of this guest locomotive and the lucky residents of the local Somerset farm can enjoy the sound effects to the full as they echo off the surrounding hillside. As can be seen from the gradient signpost, the ascent has increased to 1 in 74 although with a potential to exert a tractive effort of 32,160lb that's not going to cause any significant problems for this Crewe-built machine. Not that working with a chocolate and cream set of carriages in Great Western territory would have been a regular event, for it was a regular engine for 'The Hook Continental', a boat train from London to Harwich Parkeston Quay which connected with the ferry for the Hook of Holland. In its early days *Britannia* often hauled 'The Norfolkman' or 'The East Anglian' expresses between London and Norwich. It certainly looks to be enjoying the opportunity for a little exercise after its winter hibernation.

Leigh Wood, West Somerset Railway, Saturday 19 March 2011: Class 7F 2-8-0 53808 hauls the 16.00 Minehead to Bishops Lydeard.

As our journey following the railways through the seasons draws towards the final halt, so we see a rewarding expression of a late-afternoon's steam train climbing hard on the ascent towards Crowcombe with the Exmoor hills in the background. The steam trail tells its own story of a clean fire and well-stoked firebox with efficiently burned coal all suggesting a contented locomotive crew, for they are the heroes that coax this living machine to achieve its best potential. It's an evocative scene with nothing to suggest that we are not back in the heyday of steam and enjoying the thrall of everyday passing trains hauled by mythical hissing beasts and providing all that makes for the spectacle of railways through the changing seasons.

Chapter 5
FINALE

Crowcombe signal box and station, West Somerset Railway, 29 December 2005.

Through nature, each season expresses its colours and reveals its character, from spring's saplings surging with new life to the fading gold of late autumn's withered leaves and thence to winter's stark branches bidding a welcome to a blanket of purest white snow. Life is like that for us all and we embrace whichever stage we are at with equal joy and cheer. The seasons change gradually and suddenly we find we are immersed in the warmth or cool of the next in sequence. Steam engines on preserved lines which saw their fires kindled cautiously after the winter's break must come to a time when the daily heating of the boiler is no longer required and all goes cold … until the next season demands another impressive performance for each to show off its best potential. We can share these events, and engage in them during our journey along the rails, until such time as the winter snow bids us shelter and we then find time to contemplate all that we have relished and fondly recall the memories of each event caught within the frame of each photograph. Every picture does indeed tell its own story and we share these narratives with each other, illuminated by the glorious offerings presented by the changing seasons, looking forward to how we might seek further enrapture in the next round of their ceaseless pattern.

BIBLIOGRAPHY

Heritage Railway (magazine) (2015), Issue 202.

Ian Allan Publishing (2003) *BR Gradient Main Line Profiles*, ISBN 0 7110 0875 2.

Smith, Martin (1995) *An Illustrated History of Plymouth's Railways*, Irwell Press, ISBN 1-817608-41-4.

WEBSITES

www.naturalengland.org.uk (area profile 148: Devon Redlands)

https://ourworldindata.org/ (United Kingdom: CO2 Country Profile)